How to Survive in the
U.S.A.

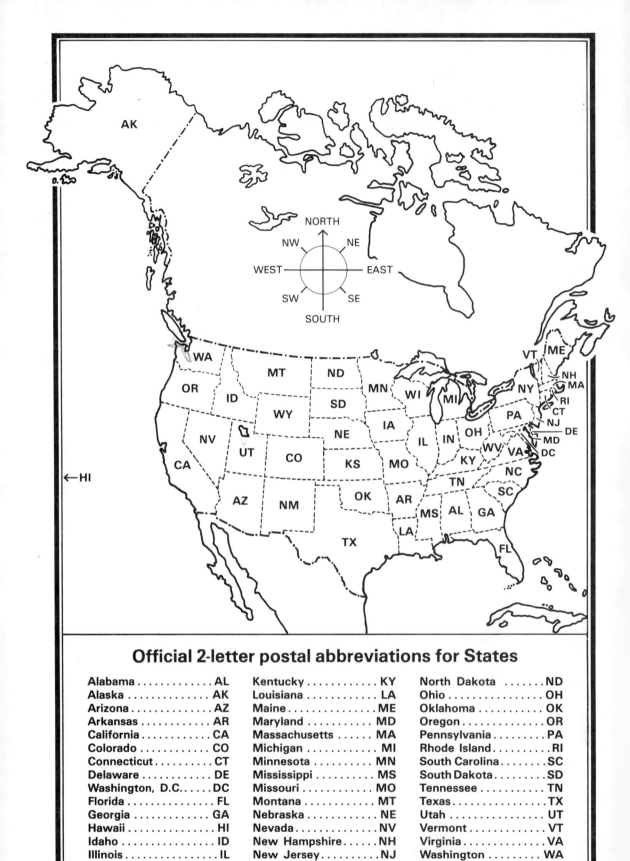

Official 2-letter postal abbreviations for States

Alabama . . . . AL	Kentucky . . . . KY	North Dakota . . . . ND
Alaska . . . . AK	Louisiana . . . . LA	Ohio . . . . OH
Arizona . . . . AZ	Maine . . . . ME	Oklahoma . . . . OK
Arkansas . . . . AR	Maryland . . . . MD	Oregon . . . . OR
California . . . . CA	Massachusetts . . . . . . MA	Pennsylvania . . . . PA
Colorado . . . . CO	Michigan . . . . MI	Rhode Island . . . . RI
Connecticut . . . . CT	Minnesota . . . . MN	South Carolina . . . . SC
Delaware . . . . DE	Mississippi . . . . MS	South Dakota . . . . SD
Washington, D.C. . . . . . DC	Missouri . . . . MO	Tennessee . . . . TN
Florida . . . . FL	Montana . . . . MT	Texas . . . . TX
Georgia . . . . GA	Nebraska . . . . NE	Utah . . . . UT
Hawaii . . . . HI	Nevada . . . . NV	Vermont . . . . VT
Idaho . . . . ID	New Hampshire . . . . . . NH	Virginia . . . . VA
Illinois IL	New Jersey . . . . NJ	Washington . . . . WA
Indiana . . . . IN	New Mexico . . . . NM	West Virginia . . . . WV
Iowa . . . . IA	New York . . . . NY	Wisconsin . . . . WI
Kansas . . . . KS	North Carolina . . . . NC	Wyoming . . . . WY

How to Survive in the U.S.A.

English for travelers and newcomers

Nancy Church and Anne Moss

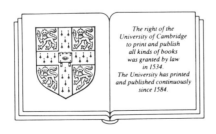

The right of the
University of Cambridge
to print and publish
all kinds of books
was granted by law
in 1534.
The University has printed
and published continuously
since 1584.

Cambridge University Press
Cambridge
New York   Port Chester   Melbourne   Sydney

Published by the Press Syndicate of the University of Cambridge
The Pitt Building, Trumpington Street, Cambridge CB2 1RP, UK
40 West 20th Street, New York, NY 10011, USA
10 Stamford Road, Oakleigh, Melbourne, 3166, Australia

First published 1983
Seventh printing 1990

Printed in the United States of America

Library of Congress cataloging in publication data
Church, Nancy

How to survive in the U.S.A.
1. English language–Text-books for foreign speakers.
2. English language–United States.
3. Readers–United States.
I. Moss, Anne.   II. Title.
PE1128.C584   1983   428.3'4   83-5185

ISBN 0 521 27206 8 book
ISBN 0 521 25111 7 cassette

British Library cataloguing in publication data
Church, Nancy

How to survive in the U.S.A.
1. English language–Text-books for foreigners
2. English language in the United States
I. Title   II. Moss, Anne
427'.973   PE1128

ISBN 0 521 27206 8 book
ISBN 0 521 25111 7 cassette

Contents

Introduction and self-study guide viii

1 *Welcome to the U.S.A.!* 2

Arriving at the airport; going through Customs; asking for and giving directions; making a connecting flight.

2 *Communicating by phone and mail* 12

Using pay phones; talking to the operator; taking and leaving messages; sending and picking up mail and telegrams.

3 *See America by rent-a-car* 22

Renting a car; asking for and giving detailed information; driving and taking care of a car.

4 *Getting around* 32

Riding public transportation in the city; turning down people's offers; reading schedules; getting from city to city by train, car, bus and plane.

5 *Places to stay* 42

Finding a room for the night; having things done for you; taking care of your clothes; finding out what's nearby.

6 *Handling your money* 52

Banking and carrying money with you – cash, credit cards and travelers checks; having money wired; asking how long something will take; going shopping.

7 *Getting something to eat* 62

Finding restaurants you like; reading the menu and ordering; asking about and describing food; going grocery shopping.

8 *In case you get sick* 72

Getting medicines and prescriptions you need; asking and talking about your health; making appointments; describing your symptoms to the doctor.

9 *Enjoying your free time* 82

Using the newspaper to find out what's happening; asking about what there is to do; reading ads and posters about concerts and other events.

10 Being a welcome guest

92

Staying at someone's home; agreeing to your host's suggestions or getting out of something politely; being invited to parties; arranging to get together again.

Teacher's guide   102

Answers and notes   107

Tapescript   125

Acknowledgments

The authors would like to thank all of our patient friends, relatives and colleagues for help with the original recording and drawings, for facilitating overseas communication, for their constructive criticism, and for still being our friends, relatives and colleagues. A special thanks goes to Peter Uhden, who especially helped get this project off the ground.

The authors and publishers are grateful to the following for permission to reproduce copyright material. U.S. Immigration and Naturalization Service (form, page 2); Portland International Airport (map, page 4); Department of the Treasury, U.S. Customs Service (form, page 6); Peter Arnold, Inc. (photos, page 5 top right and page 7); Western Union (forms, page 16 and 54); Pacific Northwest Bell (map and rates, page 20); Chrysler Corporation (photos, page 23); *This Week Magazine* (photos, pages 27 and 97); Department of Transportation, Oregon (form, page 30); Portland Taxi Cab Co. (advertisement, page 32); Trailways, Inc. (timetable, page 34); Boston MBTA (map, page 35); United Airlines (advertisement, page 37); Flamingo Hotel, Caravan Hotel (advertisements, page 42); Majestic Cleaners and Laundry, Inc. (form, page 44); *Holiday Inn* Dodge City Holidome (advertisement, page 45); Amfac Hotels (form, page 46); Westin Benson Hotel (photo, page 51 left); Barclays Bank (travelers check, page 53); Sterling Drug, Inc. (information, page 72); Baltimore Tourist Information Center (guide, page 80); Monarch Entertainment Bureau, Inc. and Avery Fisher Hall (advertisements, page 84); Warner Pacific College (photo, page 85); Seattle Opera Guild (advertisement, page 86).

Photographs on pages 5, 11, 13, 21, 24, 32, 34, 36, 41, 43, 45, 47, 51, 61, 65, 67, 73, 77, 81, 87, 91 by Nancy Church
Cartoons by Bryan Hendrix
Book design by Gavin Martin Ltd, London
Cover design by Fred Charles
Cover photo by Frederic Lewis, Inc.

Introduction

Who is this course for? **How to Survive in the U.S.A.** is an English Language Teaching book and cassette especially for people who already know some English and want to travel, vacation, study, do business, or live in the United States. It will help you to prepare for everyday language situations you may find yourself in when you are visiting the U.S. (or if you are meeting Americans* outside the U.S.)

What is in the book? There are ten units with many authentic examples of forms, documents, and written material that you may have to use or fill out in real life. There is useful information for you to look at and read in the illustrations, conversations, and texts. There are questions, answers, notes and additional recorded conversations to help you understand and test yourself.

What is on the cassette? There are 1) *Listen and read* conversations, in which you read the text after you have listened to it on the cassette and 2) *Listen and answer* and *Look and listen* conversations, which you only listen to on the cassette; we suggest that you do not read the texts of these conversations at all, but if you don't have the cassette you can find them at the back of the book in the Tapescript (pages 125–133). All the conversations are spoken by people from all parts of the U.S., from many social and cultural backgrounds in typical American accents. For review, the idioms from the *Test yourself* exercise at the end of each unit are also recorded on the cassette.

How do you use the course? You can use the book with or without a teacher, with or without a partner, and with or without the cassette. (When you see this symbol 📼 in your book, you can find the conversations on the cassette.) If you do not understand every word when you are reading or listening, don't worry. Read or listen to the part several times and it will get easier each time. Always try to get the general meaning first without using the glossaries or the dictionary – and without looking up answers to the questions. You can look them up after you understand the general idea of the conversation.

Self-study guide

Each unit has five parts. Be sure to read the directions before you start each new part.

PART I sets the scene of each unit.

A. *Study the illustration.*

B. *Read the information.*

C. *Answer the questions.*

D. *Listen and answer* presents a recorded conversation which you do not see. Read the questions first; then listen to the conversation on the cassette several times and answer the questions.

E. *Listen and read.* Without looking, just listen to the conversation on the cassette. While you are listening a second time, read the conversation. Listen and read several times until you are ready to answer the questions that follow.

F. *Answer and act.* If you are using the book with a partner, you can act out the conversation together when you see this symbol 👥. After you have played one role, trade roles (exchange parts) with your partner. If you do not have a partner, cover one of the parts and act out the other part yourself.

---

* People from the United States usually refer to themselves as "Americans." People from Canada (Canadians) and Latin America (Latin Americans – Brazilians, Mexicans, etc.) are Americans, too, but the name of the country, not the continent, is usually used to describe nationality.

PART II presents a problem for you to solve.

A. Study the illustration carefully.

B. Answer the questions. You are likely to learn some new words!

C. Look and listen presents three or four recorded conversations. Read the directions and exercises you see there first; then listen to the conversations on the cassette several times. While you are listening, look at the illustration (A) on the opposite page. Take information from the illustration or the conversations, and use it to do the exercises.

D. Problem solving gives you a chance to create your own conversations and say as much as you can. (If you do not have a partner, imagine the situation and think of what you would say.)

E. Make conversations like the ones on the cassette in *Look and listen (C)* above.

Put yourself in the place of one of the cartoon characters and act out that part. Your partner can act out the other part. Follow the instructions in the speech balloons. Here is an example of how you could do both parts of the pattern in Unit 1 (page 5) to make a conversation about *Asking and giving directions:*

– Excuse me. Could you please tell me the way to the Northwest counter?
– Sure, just go up the escalator and you'll see it on your right when you get to the top.
– Okay, let's see . . . I take the escalator up and it'll be at the top?
– Right.
– Great. Thanks.
– You're welcome.

Use some of the ideas in the directions, and then think of one or two of your own.

PART III presents more language situations.

A. Study the illustration.

B. Answer the questions.

C. Listen and read. Listen to each of the conversations on the cassette first without looking. While you are listening a second time, read the first conversation. Listen and read again, if you want to.

D. Answer the questions about the first conversation. Do the same for each of the conversations.

E. Act out the scenes with a partner, if you have one. Put yourself in the situations, and practice some of the things you heard in the conversations.

PART IV gives some useful things for you to know.

A. Read the information about traveling and living in the United States. If you have a chance, talk about this and other things you know with people interested in the same subject.

B. Compare the meanings and uses of the American and British English words. Remember that many words sound different in British English.

GLOSSARY. At the end of each unit there is a list of important words with definitions in simple English. Some words may have more than one meaning, but only meanings from the units are in the glossaries. Abbreviations (short forms) used in the glossaries are:

(n)	noun
(v)	verb
(adj)	adjective
(adv)	adverb
(prep)	preposition
(interj)	interjection
(e.g.)	for example
(etc.)	et cetera, and so on

PART V gives you a chance to see how much you've learned. First study the illustration and do the exercise, then go on to the *Activities*.

Test yourself by listening to the ten idioms on the cassette. They are expressions you will have heard in the unit. Listen several times before you do the matching exercises and answer the questions.

ANSWERS AND NOTES. Answers to all the questions and exercises are on pages 107–124. Think about your answers on your own before you look them up. Then, even if you think you know the answers, look them up, because you will often find *extra* information about the United States with the explanations and answers.

TAPESCRIPT. The texts of all the recorded conversations in *Listen and answer* and *Look and listen* are on pages 125–133. It is best to read them only after you have listened to the cassette and only if you really need to. If you do not have the cassette, read each of the conversations before you answer the questions for that part.

At the beginning of the book, you will find a map of the United States with names of all the states, the points of the compass, and the abbreviations for the states.

At the end of the book, there is a list of abbreviations often used in the U.S. There is also information about American weights and measures.

 means "work with a partner if possible."　　 means "use the cassette."

How to Survive in the U.S.A.

WELCOME TO THE U.S.A.!

PART I

A. Study this form

```
┌─────────────────────────────────────────────────┐
I-94  IMMIGRATION AND NATURALIZATION SERVICE    Form Approved
      ARRIVAL/DEPARTURE RECORD                  OMB No. 1115-077
                                                Expires 8-31-85

              WELCOME TO THE UNITED STATES

                     INSTRUCTIONS
• ALL PERSONS EXCEPT U.S. CITIZENS MUST COMPLETE THIS FORM.
  A SEPARATE FORM MUST BE COMPLETED FOR EACH PERSON IN YOUR
  GROUP.
• TYPE OR PRINT LEGIBLY WITH PEN IN ALL CAPITAL LETTERS. USE
  ENGLISH. DO NOT WRITE ON THE BACK OF THIS FORM
• This form is in two parts, an ARRIVAL RECORD (Items 1 through 7), and a DEPAR-
  TURE RECORD (Items 8 through 10). You must complete both parts. Enter exactly
  the same information in spaces 8, 9, and 10 as you enter in spaces 1, 2, and 3.
  Item 7. If you entered the United States by land, enter "LAND" in this space.
• WHEN YOU HAVE COMPLETED ALL REQUIRED ITEMS, PRESENT THIS
  FORM TO THE U.S IMMIGRATION AND NATURALIZATION INSPECTOR.
```

ADMISSION NUMBER

995-01615609   **I-94 ARRIVAL RECORD** (Rev. 1-1-83)N

1. FAMILY NAME (SURNAME) (leave one space between names)

   FIRST (GIVEN) NAME (do not enter middle name)

2. DATE OF BIRTH   3. COUNTRY OF CITIZENSHIP
   DAY | MO. | YR.
                    4. COUNTRY OF RESIDENCE (country where you live)

5. ADDRESS WHILE IN THE UNITED STATES (Number and Street)
   City   State

6. CITY WHERE VISA WAS ISSUED   7. AIRLINE & FLIGHT NO. OR SHIP NAME*

```
THIS FORM IS RE-       WARNING
QUIRED BY THE          • A nonimmigrant who accepts un-
IMMIGRATION AND          authorized employment is subject
NATURALIZATION           to deportation.
SERVICE, UNITED        IMPORTANT
STATES DEPART-         • Retain this permit in your posses-
MENT OF JUSTICE.         sion; you must surrender it when
                         you leave the U.S. Failure to do so
                         may delay your entry into the U.S.
                         in the future.
```

ADMISSION NUMBER

995-01615609

8. FAMILY NAME (SURNAME) (same as Family Name in Item 1 above)

   FIRST (GIVEN) NAME (same as First Name in Item 1 above)

9. DATE OF BIRTH   10. COUNTRY OF CITIZENSHIP (same as Item 3 above)
   (same as Item 2)
   DAY | MO. | YR.

SEE REVERSE SIDE FOR OTHER IMPORTANT INFORMATION

U.S. IMMIGRATION AND   I-94 DEPARTURE RECORD   STAPLE
NATURALIZATION SERVICE   (Rev. 1-1-83)N   HERE

For sale by the Superintendent of Documents, U.S. Government Printing Office, Washington, D.C. 20402

IMPORTANT NOTICE

• You are authorized to stay in the U.S. only until the date written on this form. To remain past this date, without permission from immigration authorities, is a violation of law.

**SURRENDER THIS PERMIT
WHEN YOU LEAVE THE UNITED STATES**

• *By sea or air*, to transportation line.
• *Over Canadian border*, to Canadian Official.
• *Over Mexican border*, at the designated location.

RECORD OF CHANGES

_____
_____
_____
_____

DEPARTURE RECORD

Port:
Date:
Carrier:
Flight No./Ship Name

B. Read

This form is called an I-94. It is the first U.S. form you see (except the ones you filled out to get your visa) and you see it whether you enter the country by air, sea or land. If you come by air, your flight attendant gives you one before the plane lands. After landing, you go to Immigration (INS), where you have to wait in line until the counter is free. Then the inspector checks your visa, completes your I-94 and staples it to your passport. Your next stop is the baggage claim area. Then you go through Customs. After that, you're on your own!

C. Answer the questions

1. Who requires this form?
2. Who has to fill it out?
3. Do you have a middle name?
4. What's your address in your country of residence?
5. Is your country of citizenship the same as your country of residence?
6. What should you do with this form while you're in the U.S.? What about when you leave?
7. Try to fill out the form.

You can look up words on page 9.

D. *Listen and answer* 📼

You will hear a conversation at a Customs desk. Listen first and then answer the questions.

1. Who are the speakers?
2. Where are they?
3. Why does the man ask so many questions?

4. Have you ever gone through U.S. Customs?
5. Where do you go after Customs?

E. *Listen and read* 📼

These people have just gone through Customs at JFK (John F. Kennedy International Airport is known as "JFK") in New York.

PETER: Well, this is it! Welcome to America!
COLLEEN: Thanks.
PETER: What are your plans?
COLLEEN: I want to go into Manhattan for a few days.
PETER: That's a good idea. It's a great town, New York. You going to take the bus to the East Side Terminal?
COLLEEN: Where?
PETER: The East Side Terminal. That's in Manhattan. There's a bus from here every half hour or so. The stop is right over there. It's the cheapest way to get there.
COLLEEN: Oh, thanks. Aren't you going to Manhattan?
PETER: No. I've got to catch a flight to L.A. in a couple of hours. I'll be taking the shuttle to LaGuardia.
COLLEEN: Did you say "shuttle"?
PETER: Mmm-hmm.
COLLEEN: What's that?
PETER: A bus that goes from JFK to LaGuardia. There are also a lot of shuttle flights to other airports and there are shuttle buses between the nine terminals here at the airport.

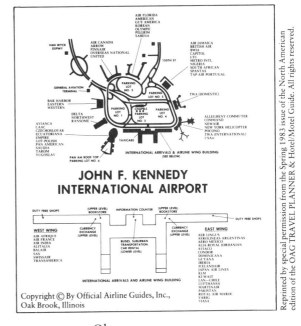

JOHN F. KENNEDY INTERNATIONAL AIRPORT

Copyright © By Official Airline Guides, Inc., Oak Brook, Illinois

COLLEEN: Oh.
PETER: Look, there's a shuttle pulling out now. Costs 75 cents, but it's still a good deal. Hey! Here comes *your* bus!

F. *Answer and act*

Listen to the conversation two or three times. Then try to answer the questions without looking at the text.

1. What are Colleen's plans?
2. What does Peter think of New York?
3. How can Colleen get to the city?
4. Where is the East Side Terminal?
5. How often do the buses go?
6. What are Peter's plans?
7. How is he going to get to LaGuardia?
8. Does he think the airport shuttles are cheap?

JFK Express Bus Stop

Bus/Train express service to Manhattan & Downtown Brooklyn.

👥 Read the conversation with a partner. Then one of you can read Peter's part while the other covers the page and plays Colleen. Trade roles.

3

PART II

A. *Study this map*

This is the terminal layout of a small American airport.

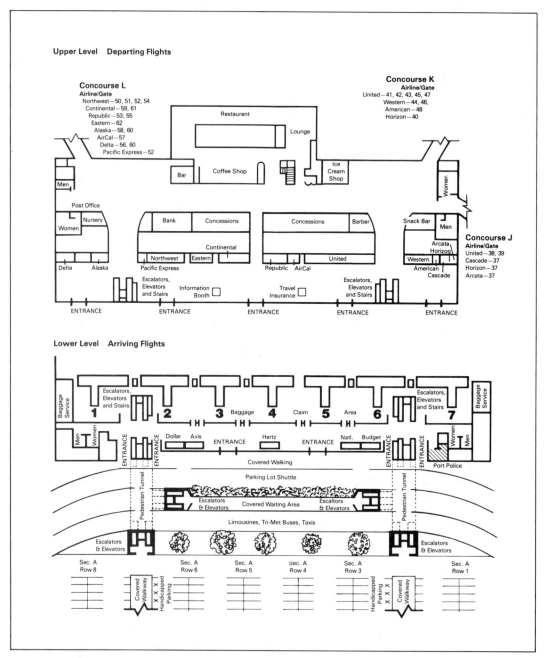

B. *Answer the questions*

1. If your flight is leaving from Gate 42, which concourse do you take?
2. When you enter the airport on the upper level, where are the nearest restrooms?
3. There's more than one place to get something to eat. Can you name two?
4. You land here and want to rent a car. Can you?
5. Do you have to walk to the parking lot? How can you get there?
6. Is this airport served by buses?

C. Look and listen 📼

You will hear three conversations at the airport. Looking at the map on page 4, figure out where the speakers are and where they have to go. Listen to the way people ask for and give directions.

1

2

3

D. Problem solving 👥

Look at the map on page 4 again. Work with a partner.

1. You arrive by taxi for an Eastern flight to Boston. Where do you go? Ask someone near the taxi stand for directions to the Eastern counter.

2. You have just picked up your luggage from baggage claim area 3. Ask someone near there how to find the restrooms.

E. Asking for and giving directions 👥

Using the following pattern and working with a partner, ask or tell the way from the information booth to the Northwest counter, Gate 39, the baggage claim area, the post office, the taxi stand, the concessions area, the restrooms, the travel insurance desk and the shuttle to the parking lot.

> Get attention and ask directions.

> Give directions.

> Repeat directions.

> Confirm or correct.

> Thank.

> Respond.

PART III

A. Study this form

You will get this form when you enter the U.S. See if you can understand it.

```
                    DEPARTMENT OF THE TREASURY
                  UNITED STATES CUSTOMS SERVICE

              CUSTOMS DECLARATION
          PRESENT TO THE IMMIGRATION AND CUSTOMS INSPECTORS

    EACH ARRIVING TRAVELER OR HEAD OF A FAMILY MUST WRITE IN THE FOL-
    LOWING INFORMATION. PLEASE PRINT
    1. FAMILY NAME            GIVEN NAME              MIDDLE INITIAL


    2. DATE OF BIRTH (Mo./Day/Yr.)      3. VESSEL, OR AIRLINE & FLT. NO.


    4. CITIZEN OF (Country)             5. RESIDENT OF (Country)


    6. PERMANENT ADDRESS



    7. ADDRESS WHILE IN THE UNITED STATES



    8. NAME AND RELATIONSHIP OF ACCOMPANYING FAMILY MEMBERS
```

FORM APPROVED
OMB NO. 48-R0386

9. Are you or anyone in your party carrying any fruits, plants, meats, other plant or animal products, birds, snails, or other live organisms of any kind? ☐ YES ☐ NO
10. Have you or anyone in your party been on a farm or ranch outside the U.S.A. in the last 30 days? ☐ YES ☐ NO
11. Are you or any family member carrying over $5000.00 (or the equivalent value in any currency) in monetary instruments such as coin, currency, traveler's checks, money orders, or negotiable instruments in bearer form? *(If yes, you must file a report on Form 4790, as required by law.)* Note: It is not illegal to transport over $5000 in monetary instruments; however, it must be reported. ☐ YES ☐ NO
12. *I certify that I have declared all items acquired abroad as required herein and that all oral and written statements which I have made are true, correct and complete.*
SIGNATURE:

NON-CITIZENS ONLY >	13. U.S. VISA ISSUED AT *(Place)*	14. VISA DATE *(Mo./Day/Yr.)*

The laws of the United States require that you declare ALL articles acquired abroad *(whether worn or used, whether dutiable or not, and whether obtained by purchase, as a gift, or otherwise)* which are in your or your family's possession at the time of arrival. **Repairs made abroad also must be declared.**

B. Answer the questions

1. Who do you have to give this form to?
2. Which members of your family do you have to list on this form?
3. Do you have to declare the amount of money you're bringing into the country?

C. Listen and read 📼

Here are two conversations that often take place at airports. The first one is at the check-in counter.

AGENT: Good morning. Your ticket, please? And set your suitcase upright and I'll check it through.

PASSENGER: Okay.

AGENT: And where would you like to sit?

PASSENGER: Make it a window seat, but if there aren't any left, I'll take an aisle seat.

AGENT: Smoking or nonsmoking?

PASSENGER: Nonsmoking.

AGENT: Uh-huh, here you go. I'm sorry, but there will be a 20-minute delay, so your flight will be boarding in about half an hour.

PASSENGER: I sure hope that's the only delay. Oh, where are my baggage claim checks?

AGENT: They're here with your ticket, sir.

PASSENGER: Great! Uh, thanks a lot.

AGENT: You're welcome. And have a nice flight.

After you get your boarding pass, you have to go through the security check.

OFFICER: Put all your carry-on luggage on the belt, ma'am.

PASSENGER: My purse and camera, too?

OFFICER: Yes, ma'am, everything. Won't hurt your film.

PASSENGER: But it's 400 ASA film.

OFFICER: Take your camera out, then, and I'll check it through by hand.

PASSENGER: Okay.

OFFICER: Thank you. Now step through here. Are you wearing any metal, ma'am?

PASSENGER: Mmm . . . why, yes, this bracelet.

OFFICER: I'm afraid you'll have to take it off, ma'am, and step through again . . . Mmm-hmm. Fine, thank you. Here's your bracelet. Have a good flight now.

PASSENGER: Okay, thanks.

 After you land, you want to fly to another city. This is a recording you might get when you try to call an airline.

Hello. TWA reservations. All our customer service lines are busy at this time. But if you hold the line, the first available agent will help you. Thank you for calling TWA.

D. *Answer the questions*

1. Where does the first passenger want to sit?
2. Why can't he board the plane now?
3. Where does the second passenger have to put her carry-on luggage?
4. Why does she have to put her purse and camera there, too?
5. Why does she have to go through security again?
6. What does the recording tell you to do? Why?

E. *Act out the scenes* 👥

1. Read the first conversation aloud several times with a partner. Trade roles.

2. Cover the text and tell exactly
   – how the check-in clerk asked where the man wanted to sit/how he answered.
   – what the check-in clerk said about boarding time.
   – how the man asked about his baggage claim checks/how the clerk answered.

3. Read the second conversation aloud with a partner. Trade roles.

4. Cover the text and tell exactly
   – how the security guard tells the woman to go through the security check.
   – how she asks the passenger if she is wearing any metal.
   – how she asks the passenger to remove her bracelet.

5. Listen to the recorded message again. What will you say when the ticket agent answers the phone? How will you say where you want to go? Practice with your partner.

PART IV

A. Read

Here are some more helpful things to know.

Airports are not always named after the city they are in. New York City has two international airports: John F. Kennedy and LaGuardia. Chicago's international airport is called O'Hare, and there's another for flights within the U.S. called Midway. The same with Washington, D.C. There's Dulles International, and National for flights within the U.S. The airport in Boston is Logan. In Seattle you'll find Seatac, from Seattle and the name of a neighboring city, Tacoma.

There are four time zones in the U.S.:

9:00 AM PACIFIC TIME

10:00 AM MOUNTAIN TIME

11:00 AM CENTRAL TIME

12:00 NOON EASTERN TIME

If you have to fly through several time zones in 12 hours or less, you may feel an upset of your body clock after the long flight. This is jet lag. Doctors say the best thing you can do is rest on the plane and perhaps have a drink of water and rest at your hotel when you arrive.

Larger airports with lots of international traffic have employees who speak languages besides English to help you, but smaller ones don't.

You can bring a total of one quart of alcoholic beverages and one carton of cigarettes (200 cigarettes) into the U.S. duty free. If you bring more, you have to pay tax.

If you lose something on the plane or can't find your baggage at the claim area, you should report it to your airline. If you lose something in the airport, you should go to the lost and found.

B. Compare

American English	British English
Excuse me?	Pardon?
purse/pocketbook/handbag	handbag
last name/family name	surname
month/day/year	day/month/year
elevator	lift
restroom	toilet
lost and found	lost property
ma'am	madam

GLOSSARY

abbreviation (n): a short form of a word

agent (n): a person who acts for or represents a company by helping customers

airline (n): an airplane business that carries passengers by air regularly

aisle (n): a long narrow space for walking, which usually divides rows of seats

alarm (n): a bell that goes off to warn people that something is wrong

alien (n): a person who is not a citizen

arrival (n): here, a plane that has just arrived

attendant (n): a person who serves customers

authorized (adj): allowed

available (adj): ready; there when it is needed

baggage claim area (n): the place to pick up suitcases and bags after a plane flight

bathroom (n): toilets

belt or *conveyor belt* (n): an endless moving band carrying things from one place to another

beverage (n): something to drink

board (v): to get on a plane, train or ship

booth (n): a small enclosed space or compartment, e.g., information booth, telephone booth

bracelet (n): an arm band; jewelry for your arm

carry-on luggage (n): a traveler's small bags carried on board a plane

check (n): a ticket given in exchange for something that will be reclaimed later, e.g., baggage check (also known as "claim check"); (v): to examine; (v): to put something in a place to be looked after, e.g., to check bags, coats, etc.; *check-in time* (n): the time at which you must report to the airline counter before the plane leaves

concessions (n): small stands or shops that sell snack foods, such as hot dogs and soft drinks, in public places

concourse (n): a hall or open public place where people pass through or gather, especially in an airport

counter (n): a narrow, high table or flat surface in a bank, shop, etc., behind which someone stands and serves customers

covered (adj): protected by a roof from the weather

currency (n): the particular type of money used in a country; *currency exchange* (n): the place for buying and selling international currency

Customs (n): the government office that examines imported goods; *customs duty* (n): tax collected on imported goods

declare (v): to tell Customs whether you are importing something that requires duty

delay (n): the amount of time that something is late

departure (n): here, a plane that is about to leave

directions (n): instructions for finding a place

elevator (n): a closet-sized room that moves up and down in a building to take people from one floor to another

escalator (n): moving steps that take people from one floor to another

figure out (v): to decide or understand about something

gate (n): that last door you pass through in an airport before you enter the airplane

illegal (adj): not lawful

Immigration (n): the government office that examines visas and passports and admits foreigners to a country

initial (n): the first letter of a name

inspector (n): a person who examines or checks, e.g., an Immigration inspector

insurance (n): a business agreement or contract in which money is paid to a company so that, if something is lost or damaged (e.g., property, life, health), the company will pay you an amount of money agreed to in the contract

L.A. (n): Los Angeles

legible (adj): readable

level (n): floor of a building

line (n): people standing behind each other; a telephone connection

locate (v): to find

lost and found (n): the office where you take things you've found and look for things you've lost

naturalization (n): the process of making a person who was born elsewhere a citizen of a country

newsstand (n): a small stand or shop that sells newspapers and magazines

nursery (n): a room where parents can take care of babies

pedestrian (n): a person walking

permanent (adj): unchanging, fixed

porter (n): a person who carries your luggage

print (v): to write in legible block letters

reservation (n): the booking or arranging of a place (airplane seat, hotel room) ahead of time

residence (n): the place and address at which a person lives; *resident* (n): a person who lives in a place and is not a visitor

restroom (n): toilets

retain (v): to keep

security (n): safety, protection from danger

shuttle (n/adj): short, connecting transportation between two places, e.g., shuttle buses between terminals, shuttle flights between nearby towns

snack bar (n): a place to eat food quickly

staple (v): to fasten papers together with a small machine using small pieces of metal

surrender (v): to give up, to hand over

terminal (n): a building where public transportation departs from or arrives

type (v): to write with a machine (typewriter)

valid (adj): officially accepted; in force; in effect

violation (n): a breaking of a law or rule

REVIEW 1

This is a map of the international airport in Boston. Study it and Unit 1 carefully before you answer the questions below.

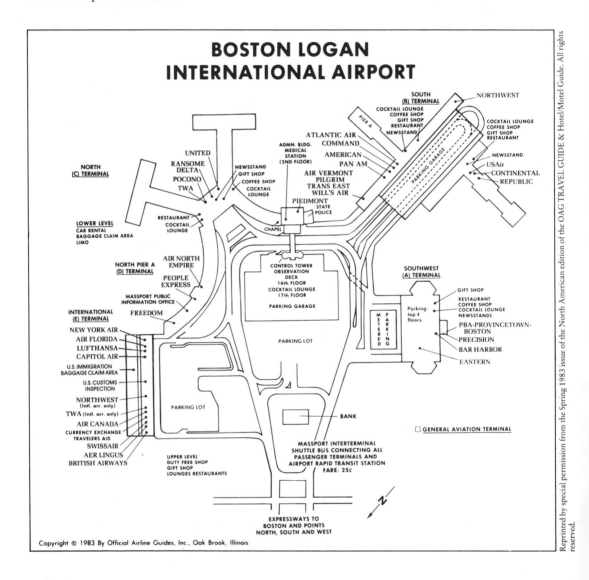

1. This is a chart showing the steps you take when you arrive in the U.S. on an international flight. Fill in the letters of the steps to the right. Find the beginning and end first.

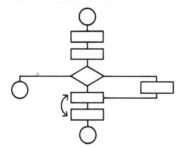

   A. Go into the city.
   B. Buy a ticket for a connecting flight.
   C. Go through Immigration.
   D. Go to South (B) Terminal.
   E. Go to the check-in counter.
   F. Departure.
   G. Go through Customs.
   H. Get your baggage.
   I. Arrival in the U.S.

2. There are four places marked on the map of Boston's international airport where you would do D, G, H and C. See if you can find them.

Activities

These are signs you can find at most airports. Why do people go to these places?

newsstand
lost and found
currency exchange
restrooms
nursery

concessions
travel insurance
post office
car rentals

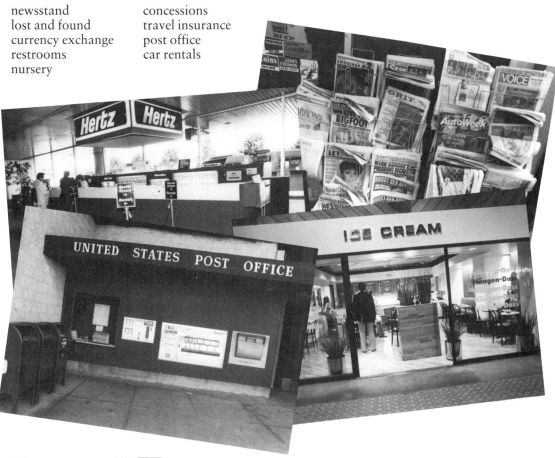

Test yourself 📼

Listen to these words and phrases from Unit 1. You may already know them, but in the conversations they have special meanings. Match them with the words on the right that mean the same. Write the letters in the blanks. (Some letters may be used more than once.)

1. .... Mmm-hmm.

2. .... Uh-huh.

3. .... Huh-uh.

4. .... You bet!

5. .... Excuse me!

6. .... Great!

7. .... You're on your own!

8. .... Hold the line.

9. .... Any time.

10. .... Excuse me?

a. Pardon me?
b. You won't have any help now.
c. I'd like to ask you something.
d. Good. Thank you.
e. Wait on the phone.
f. No.
g. You're welcome.
h. Okay.
i. Yes.

Which idioms mean Yes? Which ones mean No? Which ones would you use to respond to Thanks? To attract attention?

COMMUNICATING BY PHONE AND MAIL

PART I

A. *Study these directions*

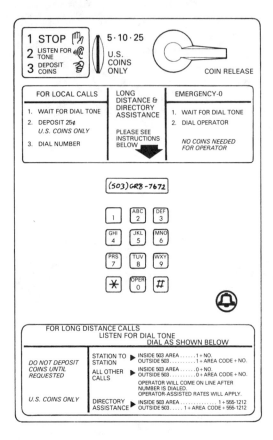

B. *Read*

In phone booths in the U.S. there are usually directions like these for using the telephone. All phone numbers have seven digits, though letters and numbers are sometimes used in combination. There may be phone books – or directories – under the telephones.

There are two main kinds of long distance calls: dial-direct and operator-assisted. You can direct dial calls in most parts of the U.S. Look in the white pages directory for long distance rates or for more information on making long distance calls. Or you can call the operator for help. If you need a phone number that's not in your phone book, call Directory Assistance.

To make a long distance call, you'll need to know the three-digit area code. Dial 1 plus the area code plus the number, and an operator or a computer voice will tell you how much money to deposit. On operator-assisted calls, the operator will ask you to deposit more money before your time is up. On dial-direct calls, you'll be cut off at the end of the time you paid for unless you put more money in the slot.

C. *Answer the questions*

1. How much does a local call cost? Is that two dimes and a nickel?
2. Will this phone take Canadian coins?
3. You deposit a quarter and then decide not to make a call. Can you get your money back? How?
4. What number do you dial in an emergency? To get information?
5. Can you direct dial a long distance call from this phone?
6. If you want to make a station-to-station call to area code 206, what do you do?
7. Do you have to pay to talk to the operator? To call the police or a doctor?

You can look up words on page 19.

D. Listen and answer 📼

You will hear three phone conversations. A man is trying to make a long distance call. He calls Directory Assistance first. Listen first and then answer the questions.

1. Who are the speakers in the three conversations?
2. What city is Vic calling from?
3. Is he calling from a private or public phone?
4. What was the problem in the second conversation?
5. What coins would you need to make a call from a pay phone in the U.S.?
6. What can you do if you can't find a phone booth?

E. Listen and read 📼

This man has just arrived at New York's JFK International Airport. He wants to call a friend in Boston to tell him when he'll be arriving, but he can't find a phone. Now he's at an information desk.

FRANK: Could you tell me where the post office is, please?

ATTENDANT: Well, the post office is down that hall. But if it's stamps you want, there's a machine right over there, but they cost more in the machine.

FRANK: Thank you, but I need a telephone.

ATTENDANT: A telephone? Well, you won't find a telephone at the post office. The phones are right over there. See the blue and white sign?

FRANK: Yes, I see. Thank you.

ATTENDANT: Hey, you got any change? You're going to need it if you want to use the phone.

FRANK: Eh, no, I haven't got any.

ATTENDANT: Well, then you'd better look for a change machine or go to the bank first. Let's see . . . let me check the time . . . Yeah, the bank's still open. Just down there and to the right.

FRANK: Thank you very much.

ATTENDANT: Yeah, it's all right.

F. Answer and act

Listen to the conversation a couple of times. Then try to answer the questions without looking at the text.

1. Where can Frank buy stamps?
2. What does he need?
3. Where are the telephones?
4. What will Frank need?
5. Is the bank still open?
6. What do you think Frank's going to do now?
7. Do you like the way the attendant acts? Why or why not?

Read the conversation with a partner. Then one of you can read the attendant's part while the other covers the page and plays Frank. Trade roles.

PART II

A. *Study this information*

This is a page of long distance rates from the Chicago phone book.

Lowest rates— dial-direct one-minute rates

Dial-direct calls are those interstate calls (excluding Alaska and Hawaii) completed from a residence or business phone without Operator assistance. The initial rate period is one minute any time of day or night. Local time where the call originates determines the rate period. Charges for additional minutes change when the call continues into a new time period.

Additional savings apply evenings, nights and weekends.

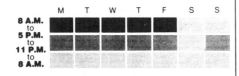

Dial-direct Sample rates from **Chicago** to:	Miles	Weekday full rate		Evening 40% discount		Night & weekend 60% discount	
		First minute	Each additional minute or fraction thereof	First minute	Each additional minute or fraction thereof	First minute	Each additional minute or fraction thereof
Atlanta, GA	598	.62	.43	.38	.26	.25	.18
Boston, MA	846	.62	.43	.38	.26	.25	.18
Denver, CO	924	.62	.43	.38	.26	.25	.18
Detroit, MI	238	.58	.39	.35	.24	.24	.16
Los Angeles, CA	1707	.64	.44	.39	.27	.26	.18
Miami, FL	1201	.64	.44	.39	.27	.26	.18
Milwaukee, WI	81	.57	.37	.35	.23	.23	.15
Minneapolis, MN	357	.59	.42	.36	.26	.24	.17
New Orleans, LA	827	.62	.43	.38	.26	.25	.18
New York, NY	711	.62	.43	.38	.26	.25	.18
St. Louis, MO	257	.58	.39	.35	.24	.24	.16
Washington, D.C.	598	.62	.43	.38	.26	.25	.18

Highest rates—Operator-assisted

Operator Assistance Charges apply to person-to-person, third number billed, public (coin) telephone, collect, requests for time and charges, certain hotel guest calls and operator-dialed Calling Card calls. These charges are never discounted and are in addition to the dial-direct rates shown in the chart to the left.

Additional minutes are at dial-direct rates and change when the call continues into a new time period.

The Operator Assistance Charges are:

Operator Station Calls

Third number billed, public (coin) phone, collect, time and charges, certain hotel guest calls, operator-dialed Calling Card calls		
	$ .75	1–10 miles
	1.10	11–22 miles
	1.55	23–3000 miles

Operator Person-to-Person Calls $3.00 all mileages

Holiday rates

New Year's Day / July 4th / Labor Day / Thanksgiving / Christmas Day. On these legal holidays, the evening rate applies all day on dial-direct calls unless a lower rate would normally apply (nights & weekends).

B. *Answer the questions*

1. What kind of call is the cheapest?
2. What kind is the most expensive?
3. When do you get the largest discount on dial-direct calls?
4. What are some kinds of calls the operator has to help you with?
5. When you direct dial a call, how much time do you have to pay for?
6. How much time do you have to pay for on an operator-assisted call?
7. Is there ever a discount on operator-assisted calls?
8. You make a person-to-person call to Denver at 9:00 p.m. Chicago time. How much does it cost you?
9. Look at question 8 again. If you had direct dialed, how much would it have cost?

C. Look and listen

You will hear four conversations on the phone. Listen to the way people ask for information and take and leave messages. Listen to the conversations again and figure out who the speakers are, and whether or not they know each other.

1. The lady in the first conversation couldn't find the rates for Miami. Look on page 14 and see if you can.

2. The woman in the second conversation made a business call, but couldn't get through to Mr. Bixby. Write the message for him.

3. Tod's mother was casual with Wally. Write the message for Tod.

4. Make up a message to leave on the tape "at the sound of the tone".

D. Problem solving

Call Directory Assistance and ask for the number of someone in another part of the country. Spell their name for the operator, using this alphabet. (Say "V" as in Victor, for example.) Get their number and the area code and repeat it, just to be sure you got it right.

"A" as in Alice	J – James	S – Samuel
B – Bertha	K – Kate	T – Thomas
C – Charles	L – Lewis	U – Utah
D – David	M – Mary	V – Victor
E – Edward	N – Nellie	W – William
F – Frank	O – Oliver	X – X-ray
G – George	P – Peter	Y – Young
H – Henry	Q – Quaker	Z – Zebra
I – Ida	R – Robert	

E. Taking and leaving messages

Using the following pattern and working with a partner, take or leave messages for the following people: Mrs. Collins at National Bank in San Diego; Mr. Jones at Bell Telephone; your tennis partner, Judy; your dinner date for tomorrow, Mark; and the woman you just met last Wednesday, Carol Smith.

Say hello.

Say he or she isn't available.

Repeat the message and say goodbye.

Say hello and ask for someone.

Leave a message.

Say goodbye.

PART III

A. Study this telegram form

In the U.S. you cannot send telegrams from the post office. You go to a telegraph office, such as Western Union. This is a form you could fill out if you wanted to send a telegram. See if you can understand it.

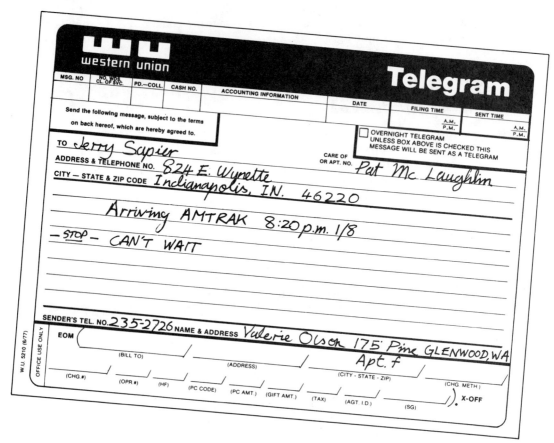

B. Answer the questions

1. What information do you have to put on this form?
2. Who is sending this telegram? What does she say?
3. What is the recipient's name? Does he have his own address?
4. Is Valerie looking forward to seeing Jerry? How can you tell?
5. Think of a message you could send and write your own telegram.

C. Listen and read ⊟

Some people are waiting in line at the post office in a small town in Tennessee. The first one wants to pick up his mail.

CLERK: Next, please.
RICHARD: Hi! They told me over at the Morningside post office that I could pick up my mail here. Do you have the General Delivery letters?
CLERK: Yes, we do. Can you show me some ID?
RICHARD: Yeah, I think I have something with my picture on it . . . Here's my driver's license.
CLERK: Richard Stephens . . . Okay, Richard, just a minute . . . Well, you hit it lucky today – three letters for you!
RICHARD: All right, thanks a lot!

The second person has some packages she wants to mail.

CLERK: Next.

JANET: Hi! I want to mail this box of books to Japan. It's okay if it's sealed, isn't it?

CLERK: Sure. But there's an eleven pound weight limit, and that box looks pretty big.

JANET: Oh, it weighs less than eleven pounds.

CLERK: Okay. You want it to go surface, I take it? Let's see . . . yup, ten pounds even. Wait a minute! This isn't labeled right.

JANET: What's wrong with it?

CLERK: Where's the return address?

JANET: On the other side.

CLERK: The sender's return address has to go here in the upper left hand corner, and, look here – you forgot your zip code.

JANET: Okay. I'll write it in. This other package here has to get to Lyons as soon as possible.

CLERK: Where's that?

JANET: In southern France.

CLERK: Well, express is the fastest to Europe, but it's very expensive. Airmail's bad enough, even for small packets, but that's over two pounds, so it'll have to go as a parcel, and that costs a lot more.

JANET: It's over two pounds, I know . . . How long does airmail take?

CLERK: Oh, about a week or ten days.

JANET: Yeah, that's okay . . . I'll send it airmail after all. And I'd like it registered and insured for $50.

CLERK: Okay, fill out this form, then.

D. Answer the questions

1. Why does Richard have to show the postmaster an ID to get his mail?
2. What's the difference between surface, air, express and registered mail?
3. Why doesn't Janet send the second package by surface mail?

E. Act out the scenes

1. Read the first conversation several times with a partner. Trade roles.

2. Tell your partner exactly
   – how Richard asked if the clerk had the General Delivery letters.
   – how the clerk asked Richard for some ID.
   – how the clerk told Richard he was lucky.

3. Read the second conversation aloud several times with a partner. Trade roles.

4. Cover the text and tell your partner exactly
   – how Janet said she wanted to mail a box of books.
   – how she asked the clerk if the box could be sealed.
   – how the clerk told Janet there is a weight limit.
   – how the clerk told Janet how long airmail takes.

5. Listen to the second conversation again and take notes on what the clerk says. Then act out the situation using your notes.

PART IV

A. Read

Here are some more helpful things to know.

Phone books have white, blue and yellow pages. The white pages list people with phones by last name. The blue pages contain numbers of city services, government services, and public schools. Businesses and professional services are listed in a special classified directory – the Yellow Pages.

The area covered by one area code may be small or large. For example, New York City has one area code, but so does the whole state of Oregon. There is an area code map of the U.S. and Canada in the front of the white pages.

Pay phones have numbers in the U.S. This means you can arrange to call a friend at a phone booth. Or if you are making a long distance call and run out of money, give the number on your phone to the person you're talking to. Then hang up the receiver and they can call you back.

If you make a long distance call and get a wrong number, call the operator and explain what happened. This means that you can make the call again to the right number without having to pay more money; or you can have the phone company mail you a

credit coupon that has the same value as the phone call.

Some companies advertise a service called WATS. You can dial a special number without a long distance charge. These are called "toll-free numbers" and the area code for all of them is 800. WATS means Wide Area Telephone Service.

The U.S. Postal Service has competitors. Courier services send or transmit messages; parcels and freight are delivered by a number of companies. Check the Yellow Pages for details.

There are two ways of sending things safely through the post office: registered and certified mail. Certified is much cheaper. Ask at the post office for more information.

You can have mail sent to you General Delivery in any town. It will be held ten days, or up to a month if the sender writes "Please hold 30 days" on the envelope. Using the zip code will speed up delivery.

Remember, you cannot usually send telegrams or make telephone calls from U.S. post offices.

B. Compare

American English	British English
to call (up)	to ring (up)
person-to-person call	personal call
to call collect	to reverse the charges
to connect	to put through
long distance call	trunk call
phone booth	phone kiosk/phone box
area code	STD code
directory assistance/ information	directory enquiries
busy	engaged
to wait in line/line up	to queue up
zip code	post code
unlisted	ex-directory

GLOSSARY

advertise (v): to make known to the public, as in a movie, newspaper, etc.

answering machine (n): a machine that answers the phone, plays a recorded message and may record a caller's message

apply (v): to be in effect

area code (n): three numbers that must be used in front of the phone number when making a long distance telephone call

bill (n): a list of things bought, or money owed; (v): to send someone a list of things they bought and ask for payment of money owed

care of (n): at the address of; also "c/o"

casual (adj): relaxed, informal, easygoing

certified mail (n): a postal service that gives the sender a record of sending a piece of mail

charge (n): the price asked or paid for something; (v): to ask in payment

check (v): to put a mark in a box; to look and see

classified (adj): arranged or divided into different groups

coin release (n): a little lever or bar on a phone, which you push down to get your money back

collect call (n): a long distance telephone call in which the person you are calling pays

competitor (n): a company that does the same type of business your company does

coupon (n): a ticket that is worth a certain amount of money or that gives you a discount when buying something

courier service (n): a company that delivers important letters or messages very fast

credit (n): permission to borrow money that a bank or store gives to a customer if they think the customer has enough income, is honest, and will repay his debts. A *credit card* is often given to the customer to show that he has credit. Also, credit can be a way of paying money owed to someone without giving him cash.

credit card (n): a numbered card given by a bank or company with which you can buy an item or a service and pay for it later

cut off (v): to have a telephone connection disconnected or broken

date (n): a person of the opposite sex who you have arranged to meet socially

deposit (v): to put money in the phone

dial (n): the face or wheel on the front of a telephone; (v): to choose the number on a phone, also on a push-button phone

dial direct (v): to dial a long distance call without the operator's help

directory (n): the book listing telephone numbers by customer's name

discount (n): an amount off a regular price; for example, a 35% discount means you pay 65% of the regular price

emergency (n): an unexpected situation that is serious or dangerous and that requires immediate action or help

even (adv): exactly

freight (n): items too large to be sent by mail

General Delivery letters (n): mail that the post office holds for people to come in and pick up; "poste restante"

hang up (v): what you do with the telephone receiver after you say goodbye

ID, identification (n): an official paper that proves who a person is

initial (adj): beginning, starting

interrupt (v): to break in on what someone else is saying

label (v): to fix or write information, such as name and address, on something

license (n): a permit allowing you to do something

long distance call (n): a call outside of the area you are calling from

operator (n): the person who helps you make long distance phone calls

packet (n): a small package

parcel (n): a package

pay phone (n): a public phone where you pay for each call before or immediately after you make it

person-to-person call (n): a long distance call made with the operator's help, in which you only want to speak to a specific person. If that person isn't there, there is no charge for the call

pretty (adj): rather

rate (n): a charge

receiver (n): the part of the telephone that you hold to your ear

recipient (n): a person who gets something in the mail

registered mail (n): a letter or package that carries a number that is recorded in the post office so that it can be found if it doesn't arrive at the correct address

request (v): to ask or demand politely

return address (n): the address of the sender

run out (v): to have no more

savings (n): money saved

seal (v): to fasten or close with tape or glue

sender (n): the person who mails something

slot (n): a narrow opening in which you put coins

station-to-station call (n): a long distance call in which you will speak to anyone who answers

subject to (adj): under certain conditions

surface (adj): mail sent surface goes by train, truck or ship

terms (n): the conditions of an agreement

tied up (adj): busy

time and charge (n): the operator tells you the length of time you talked and how much it cost when your long distance call is ended. The cost is charged to the owner of the phone

toll (n): a charge made for a long distance call; *toll-free* (adj): without a toll

tone (n): a sound

transmit (v): to send a message by wire or radio

zip code (n): five numbers (in future, nine) that are used after an address in the U.S. Each post office in the country has a different zip code.

REVIEW 2

This is a map of the area codes for telephoning in the U.S. Study it and Unit 2 carefully before you answer the questions below.

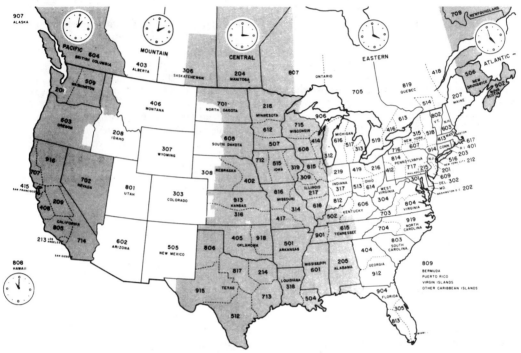

1. You want to make a long distance call from Portland to a friend in Atlanta, Georgia. Write out the steps you would go through. Use these words: area code; dial; receiver; slot; coins.
2. Find the area code you need.

3. Figure out when it would be cheapest to call your friend. How long could you talk for two dollars?
4. If you can't reach your friend by phone, how else could you get a message to them?

SAMPLE RATES FROM PORTLAND TO:	DIAL-DIRECT					
	WEEKDAY FULL RATE		EVENING DISCOUNT		NIGHT & WEEKEND DISCOUNT	
	First Minute	Each Additional Minute	First Minute	Each Additional Minute	First Minute	Each Additional Minute
Anchorage, Ak.	$.64	$.46	$.45	$.33	$.29	$.21
Atlanta, Ga.	.66	.46	.43	.30	.26	.18
Boston, Mass.	.66	.46	.43	.30	.26	.18
Chicago, Ill.	.64	.44	.42	.29	.26	.18
Dallas, Tex.	.64	.44	.42	.29	.26	.18
Denver, Colo.	.64	.44	.42	.29	.26	.18
Hawaii (All Cities)	.66	.48	.46	.34	.30	.22
Kansas City, Kan.	.64	.44	.42	.29	.26	.18
Los Angeles, Cal.	.61	.42	.40	.27	.24	.17
Miami, Fla.	.66	.46	.43	.30	.26	.18
Phoenix, Ariz.	.64	.44	.42	.29	.26	.18
San Francisco, Cal.	.61	.42	.40	.27	.24	.17
Seattle, Wash.	.53	.37	.34	.24	.21	.15
Washington, D.C.	.66	.46	.43	.30	.26	.18

Activities

Explain the difference between the following words:

white pages/Yellow Pages   dime/quarter
area code/zip code   packet/parcel
station-to-station/person-to-person   operator-assisted/dial-direct
airmail/surface mail   express/registered

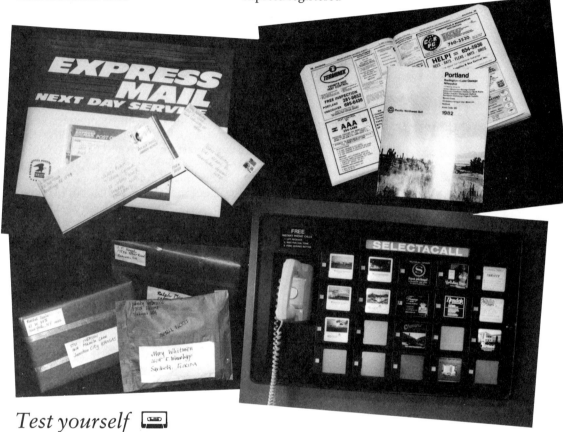

Test yourself

Listen to these words and phrases from Unit 2. You may already know them, but in the conversations they have special meanings. Match them with the words on the right that mean the same. Write the letters in the blanks.

1. .... I'll get back to you.
2. .... Your time is up.
3. .... Will do.
4. .... It's pretty big.
5. .... Hang up.
6. .... You'll be cut off.
7. .... Far out!
8. .... I ran out of money.
9. .... What's up?
10. .... I take it?

a. The phone connection will be broken.
b. I suppose?
c. What do you want to say?
d. I'll call you again.
e. It's kind of big.
f. Okay, I'll do it.
g. You have no more time.
h. Put the phone down.
i. Wonderful!
j. I don't have any more money.

Which idioms would you use in a phone conversation with the operator?

SEE AMERICA BY RENT-A-CAR

PART I

A. Study this advertisement

Weekly Rate

500 Free Miles

Only $70.00

Daily Rate

$8.00 PER DAY   **10¢**   PER MILE

½ Price Gas

"Laugh at gas prices! Buy gas any place you want. Just bring in your receipt and we'll credit you ½ the cost!"

* Gallon limit subject to change, details posted at our office.

FREE AIRPORT SHUTTLE. FREE SHUTTLE SERVICE TO GARAGES THAT DISPLAY THE UGLY DUCKLING SIGN.

B. Read

This is a car rental advertisement you would find in a phone book if you looked under Car Rentals in the Yellow Pages. The two largest American car rental companies, Hertz and Avis, have offices all over the U.S., with counters at most airports and in many international cities. Other national car rental companies you can find at airports, such as Thrifty, National, Budget or Dollar, have offices in other countries too, so you may want to reserve a car through your travel agent in your own country.

In order to rent a car, you have to have a major credit card, such as MasterCard or Visa, or a credit card with the company itself. Without a credit card you may have to pay a very high deposit on the car.

It is also possible to rent used cars rather than new ones. Rent-A-Junker and Ugly Duckling, which have offices in 40 states, are two of the many used car rental companies. Their rates are often lower and they don't always demand a credit card. Sometimes they have special offers that make the total cost of renting a car even lower.

C. Answer the questions

1. If you don't have a credit card, will it be easier to rent a car from Hertz or Ugly Duckling?
2. Name some other rent-a-car companies.
3. If you want to drive a new car, which companies should you go to?
4. Which is cheaper at Ugly Duckling – the daily or the weekly rate?
5. Does Ugly Duckling have a special offer? Explain it.
6. You rent an Ugly Duckling car and drive it for three days. Which rate applies? How much do you have to pay per mile?
7. You have the car a week and drive 800 miles. Do you have to pay more than $70? Why?
8. Does Ugly Duckling have a counter at the airport?
9. How can you get to the Ugly Duckling city office from the airport?

You can look up words on page 29.

D. Listen and answer

You will hear a conversation that takes place at a car rental agency at the airport. Listen first and then answer the questions.

1. Who are the speakers?
2. What did Ms. Ferris want to do?
3. When will she return the car?
4. How does she pay?

5. What are things to consider when renting a car?
6. What do you do about insurance?

E. Listen and read

This man just arrived at a car rental office to pick up the car he reserved.

AGENT: Good morning. May I help you?

TAYLOR: Yes, my name's Taylor. I reserved a car.

AGENT: Yes, Mr. Taylor, here's your reservation for a Ford Granada. Did you want any extra insurance on that?

TAYLOR: I don't know . . . what kind of coverage do you offer?

AGENT: Liability is included, and we have $350 deductible collision, so if you have an accident, you pay us $350. For a charge of $5 a day, we'll waive your responsibility for collision damage. It's sort of like additional coverage.

TAYLOR: Well, $5 a day sounds reasonable, if I don't have to pay anything in case the car is damaged.

AGENT: All right . . . how about personal accident?

TAYLOR: Well, I don't know. What does it cover?

AGENT: Medical expenses up to $2,000 for the driver and each passenger in case of accident, and, well, here . . . this folder will describe it for you.

TAYLOR: Mmm . . . no, I don't think this'll be necessary, thanks.

AGENT: All right, here's your rental agreement. Just sign here, please.

F. Answer and act

Listen to the conversation two or three times. Take notes on what the agent explains about insurance. Then try to answer the questions from your notes.

1. What arrangement did Mr. Taylor make with the car rental company?
2. What kind of coverage does the company include in its agreement?
3. What does "$350 deductible collision" mean? What is the $5 a day for?

4. What does "personal accident" cover?
5. Does Mr. Taylor want any extra insurance? If so, what?
6. What does the agent ask him to do with the rental agreement?

♦♦ Read the conversation with a partner. Then one of you can read the agent's part while the other covers the page and plays Mr. Taylor. Trade roles.

PART II

A. *Study this form*

The car rental agent fills out this form for you.

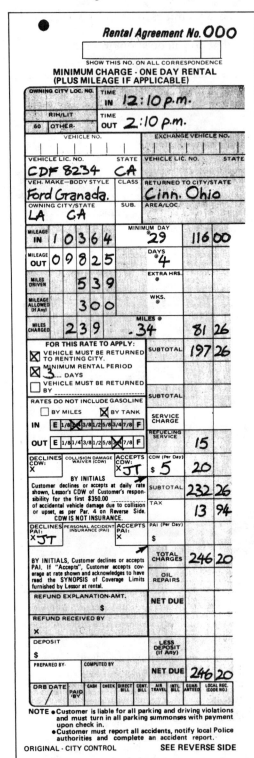

B. *Answer the questions*

1. What is the rate per mile? Per day?
2. Does the rental agreement allow the customer any free mileage? How much?
3. How full was the gas tank when the customer picked the car up? When he brought it back?
4. Did he ask for extra personal insurance?
5. Did he make a deposit when he rented the car?
6. The customer got a parking ticket in Columbus. What should he do with it?
7. Who is the lessor?
8. Who can drive this car?
9. Explain in simple English the terms the customer agrees to in the "small print" in this agreement.

Customer authorizes Lessor to process a credit card voucher (if applicable) in Customer's name for charges. Vehicle shall NOT be operated by any person except Customer and the following Authorized Operators who must be validly licensed to drive and have Customer's prior permission: persons 21 or over who are members of Customer's immediate family and permanently reside in Customer's household; the employer, partner, executive officer, or a regular employee of Customer; additional authorized operator(s) approved by Lessor in writing.
Customer agrees not to permit use of Vehicle by any other person without obtaining Lessor's prior written consent.
THE VEHICLE IS RENTED UPON THE CONDITIONS SHOWN ON THIS PAGE AND UPON THE REVERSE HEREOF. CUSTOMER REPRESENTS HE HAS READ, UNDERSTANDS AND AGREES WITH THE CONDITIONS. ALSO SEE NOTE BELOW.

X Specimen Void

C. Look and listen 📼

You will hear three conversations that take place at a car rental counter. Listen to the way people ask for information about their rental agreement. Looking at the form on page 24, find the information they're talking about and decide what the customer has to do.

1. What if the car breaks down? Who do you call and what will they do for you?

2. What about insurance? Which boxes can you check and what kind of insurance are you getting if you accept?

3. If there's an accident, who do you have to notify? What do you have to fill out? What about if you get a parking ticket?

D. Problem solving 👥

You have decided to join a car rental club. You work for the ATS Company and want to rent a standard size Buick several times a month over a two year period. Fill out this application with the help of an agent.

The CAR RENT club

Complete application and return.
Postage is pre-paid. Please print or type.

Check the car size you prefer:
___ Compact   ___ Intermediate   ___ Full-Size

Last Name _____

First Name _____

Home Phone Number
(include area code) _____

Your Corp-Rate identification sticker entitles you to low unlimited mileage rates.
Please circle the one credit card you prefer to use for payment:

American Express, BankAmericard/Visa,
Carte Blanche,
Diners Club,

Credit card number _____

Date of Birth: Month ___ Day ___ Year ___

Home Address _____

City _____ State _____ Zip _____

Company Name _____

Company Phone Number
(include area code) _____

Driver's License Number
(include letters) _____

State/Country of Issuance _____

Expiration Date: Month ___ Day ___ Year ___

■ CAR RENT ■
rent a car

E. Asking for and giving detailed information 👥

Using the following pattern and working with a partner, ask for or give information. Ask about car sizes, prices, free mileage, parking tickets, accidents, car trouble, personal accident insurance, liability and drivers other than you.

Ask for information.

Give information.

Thank.

RENT A CAR

		WEEKLY RATES
A.	Economy	$79
B.	Midsize	$119
C.	Midsize plus	$149
D.	Standard	$159
E.	Pick-up	$139
F.	Van	$169
G.	Trailer	$179

PART III

A. Study this picture

This shows a car with its parts identified.

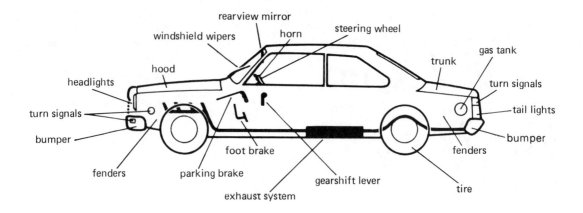

B. Answer the questions

Below are descriptions of some car parts. Read each one, then find the part described on the drawing.

1. You turn these on at night.
2. You use these when it rains.
3. You put gas in it.
4. You use it to stop.
5. You set it before you get out of the car to keep the car from moving.
6. You use these when you want to go left or right.
7. These cover the tires.
8. You can put luggage in here.
9. These tell other drivers when you are braking.
10. You use this to see cars behind you.
11. This covers the engine.
12. You use this to warn other drivers.
13. You move this with your right hand when you change gears.
14. You turn this to steer the car.

C. Listen and read 📼

Here are three conversations about driving. The first two take place at gas stations.

ATTENDANT 1: What'll it be today, ma'am?
DRIVER 1: Ten dollars worth of unleaded, please. Here's the key to the tank.
ATTENDANT 1: Comin' right up . . . Check the oil for you today?
DRIVER 1: Yes, please, and could you get the windshield, too?
ATTENDANT 1: Sure thing. Open the hood for me, will you? There's a lever inside there.
DRIVER 1: Oh, yes, of course.
ATTENDANT 1: Okay, ma'am, that'll be ten dollars.
DRIVER 1: Here you are.
ATTENDANT 1: Thanks. You take care now.

DRIVER 2: Hmm. Prices at this station aren't too bad. They've got regular, unleaded and premium. Wow, they even have gasohol!
ATTENDANT 2: What can I do for you?
DRIVER 2: Fill 'er up, and check the tires, will you? I think they're low on air.
ATTENDANT 2: Sorry, you're at the mini-serve island. When you're here, I just pump gas. You can drive over to the full-serve island and I'll do it, but the gas will cost you more.
DRIVER 2: Oh, okay, never mind. I'll check them myself. Go ahead and fill it.

Two cars have had a small accident. The drivers are talking to . . . well, arguing with each other.

BILL: Idiot! Why didn't you watch where you were going?

HANK: You should've let me over! Couldn't you see me signaling? Don't you even know how to drive? Look at my fender!

BILL: Your fender! Big deal! Look at these scratches all down the side of mine! It's only six months old! You'll pay for this!

LINDA: Hey, man! What's the matter? Move these cars over so the rest of us can get by!

HANK: All right, all right, keep your shirt on! We'll get out of the way . . .

BILL: Oh, no you don't. Leave the car where it is. Give me your address before you get in there. Write it down on this piece of paper and I'll move *my* car.

LINDA: Didn't see the yield sign, huh? Men drivers . . .!

HANK: Ah, lay off. It could have happened to you.

BILL: And you, lady, could I have your address, too? You were a witness, right?

LINDA: Who, me? Oh, no. Are you kidding? I didn't see it happen. You'll have to find somebody else.

D. Answer the questions

1. What does the first attendant do for the driver?
2. What kind of service does the customer get there?
3. What two things does the driver ask the second attendant to do?
4. Does the attendant do both of them?
5. Whose fault does the accident seem to be?
6. What damage was done to Hank's car? What about Bill's?
7. What does Linda want the men to do? What does Bill want her to do?

E. Act out the scenes

1. Read the first and second conversations several times with a partner. Trade roles.

2. Cover the text and act out the conversations. Be sure to say the exact words used when
    – the attendants said hello.
    – the customers ordered.
    – the attendants replied.

3. Read the third conversation several times with a partner. Trade roles.

4. Cover the text and tell your partner exactly
    – how Bill first spoke to Hank.
    – how Bill said Hank would have to pay.
    – how Linda told Bill and Hank to move their cars.
    – how Bill asked for Hank's address.
    – how Bill asked for Linda's address.
    – how Linda refused to get involved.

PART IV

A. Read

Here are some more helpful things to know.

Americans like to do business without leaving their cars. You'll see drive-in banks, drive-in restaurants, drive-in churches and drive-in movies.

When driving in the U.S., it's a good idea to have an international drivers' license if you don't have a state license. Each of the fifty states has its own traffic laws. (For example, in some states drivers can pump their own gas at "self-serve islands," while in others this is not allowed.) Drivers are expected to know and understand the laws even if they don't live in the state. Get information when you cross the border into a state at a tourist information center.

There is a national speed limit of 55 miles per hour, or about 80 kilometers per hour. Americans usually start and stop slowly and are generally polite about letting cars enter busy streets. They usually stop for people who are walking to let them cross the street. In many states you may turn right after stopping at a corner, even if there is a red light. On some roads there may be a minimum speed.

If you rent a car, ask the company what to do in case your car breaks down. Some companies will ask you to call a special number. Others will want you to have the car repaired. They will deduct the cost of the repair from your bill.

"Mileage" can mean two things. It may mean the total number of miles a car has been driven, as it does on the form on page 24. We say "This car has 10,000 miles on it; it has low mileage." On the other hand, "gas mileage" is the number of miles a car can travel on one U.S. gallon of gas. For example, a big car that gets 25 miles to the gallon gets very good mileage. A small economy car should get at least 35 miles to the gallon when it's new.

If you want to rent a vehicle you can sleep in, you should ask about RV's, recreational vehicles. You don't need a car to pull an RV — you can drive it! Yet it's as big as a house trailer. You can also rent a camping trailer.

B. Compare

American English	British English
to rent	to hire
fender	wing/mud guard
hood	bonnet
windshield	windscreen
trunk	boot
tire	tyre
license plate	number plate
gas/gasoline	petrol
gas station	filling station
trailer/camper/mobile home	caravan
underpass	subway
sidewalk	pavement
detour	diversion

GLOSSARY

agency (n): a business that brings people in touch
  with others or with products

argue (v): to disagree strongly with words

brake (n): the system that stops or slows a vehicle;
  (v): to use the brake to slow a vehicle

cash (n): paying with money in the form of coins
  and banknotes instead of with a credit card

charge (n): paying by using a credit card

collision (n): a crash; (adj): a type of insurance
  that pays for repair of damage from collision

consider (v): to think something over

coverage (n): the amount of protection that
  insurance provides

daily (adj/adv): every day

deduct (v): to take away (an amount) from a
  total; *deductible* (n/adj): in insurance, the
  money a customer must pay before the
  insurance pays the cost of a loss

deposit (n): a pre-payment of money as a sign that
  the rest will be paid later

display (v): to show

duckling (n): a baby duck; "The Ugly Duckling"
  is the title of a children's story

exhaust (n): the smoke and gases that come out of
  a car's engine; *exhaust system* (n): the pipes
  that allow unwanted gasses to escape from the
  car's engine

folder (n): a folded piece of paper with
  information about something; brochure

full-serve island (n): at a gas station, the row of
  pumps where the attendant washes
  windshields, checks the oil and tires, etc., and
  where gas costs more

gallon (n): a measure for liquids, four quarts; 3.8
  liters

garage (n): a business which repairs cars; a
  building to park a car in

gas (n): common short form for "gasoline," the
  fuel that a car uses

gasohol (n): gas mixed with alcohol

gears (n): the mechanical system in a car that
  changes the power from the engine into
  forward motion, making the wheels turn

guarantee (v): to ensure or promise that
  something is of good quality

hey (interj): a shout used to call attention or
  express surprise or interest

hood (n): the cover over a car's engine

idiot (n): a foolish person; a person who is not at
  all intelligent

junker (n): an old car in bad condition

kid (v): to joke; to pretend or deceive in a playful
  manner

lessor (n): a person who rents something to
  another person; *lessee* (n): a person who rents
  something

lever (n): a bar or stick that is pulled or pushed to
  cause something to work

liability (n): the responsibility or fault for
  something; a debt; *liable* (adj): legally
  responsible for a debt

lic. no. (n): abbreviation for "license number,"
  the registration number of your car

merge (v): two traffic lanes join to form one

mileage (n): the number of miles on a car; the
  number of miles per gallon a car gets

mph (n): abbreviation for "miles per hour"

mini-serve island (n): at a gas station, the row of
  pumps where gas is cheaper, but less service is
  available

net (n): amount; price remaining to be paid

notify (v): to inform or tell a person

obtain (v): to get

per (prep): for each

post (v): to make public by putting on a wall

premium (adj): the better type of gas

pre-paid (adj): paid for before

prior (to) (prep): before

pump (n): a machine that moves liquids upward;
  (v): to move liquids, air or gas, by using a pump

receipt (n): a written statement that you have
  received or paid money

refund (n): money returned to you when you have
  paid too much

regular (adj): the normal type of gas

rental (n): a sum of money to be paid for using
  something

RR (n): railroad, railway

satisfaction (n): the state of being pleased

scratch (n): a mark or injury to a surface made by
  something rough or pointed

shift (v): to change from one gear to another

signal (v): to give a sound or visual sign as a
  warning

specimen (n): a typical example

summons (n): a demand to come to court

technical language (n): specialized words and
  terms

ticket (n): a printed notice of an offense against
  driving laws

trailer (n): a wheeled vehicle pulled by a car,
  bicycle or truck

unleaded (adj): gas with no lead

U turn (n): a 180° turn

vehicle (n): something with wheels that can carry
  or move people or things

violation (n): the breaking of a traffic law

void (adj): not valid

waive (v): to give up a claim; *waiver* (n): an
  official statement waiving a claim

witness (n): a person who sees something happen,
  such as an accident

yield (v): to make way for another person or
  driver

REVIEW 3

This is part of an accident form. Study it and Unit 3 carefully before you answer the questions below.

TO BE COMPLETED BY DRIVER OF VEHICLE NUMBER 1

TYPE OF ACCIDENT
(MARK AS MANY AS APPLY)

IF COLLISION
ACCIDENT INVOLVED:

- ☐ ONE OTHER VEHICLE
- ☒ TWO OR MORE VEHICLES
- ☐ PEDESTRIAN
- ☒ PARKED VEHICLE
- ☐ RAILROAD TRAIN
- ☐ PEDAL CYCLIST
- ☐ MOTOR CYCLIST
- ☐ ANIMAL
- ☐ FIXED OBJECT
- ☐ OTHER

IF NON-COLLISION
ACCIDENT WAS DUE

- ☐ TO OVERTURNING
- ☐ OTHER REASON

DRIVER NO. 1 (YOU) INTENDED TO:
(MARK ONE)

- ☒ GO STRAIGHT AHEAD
- ☐ LEAVE DRIVEWAY
- ☐ MAKE RIGHT TURN
- ☐ REMAIN STOPPED IN TRAFFIC
- ☐ MAKE LEFT TURN
- ☐ START IN TRAFFIC LANE
- ☐ SLOW OR STOP
- ☐ ENTER PARKED POSITION
- ☐ MAKE U TURN
- ☐ LEAVE PARKED POSITION
- ☐ BACK UP
- ☐ REMAIN PARKED
- ☐ ENTER DRIVEWAY
- ☐ OVERTAKE AND PASS

YOUR VEHICLE
(NO. 1) (MARK ONE)

- ☒ PASSENGER CAR
- ☐ TRUCK TRACTOR AND SEMI-TRAILER
- ☐ CAR AND TRAILER
- ☐ OTHER TRUCK COMBINATION
- ☐ TAXICAB
- ☐ FARM TRACTOR AND/OR FARM EQUIPMENT
- ☐ BUS
- ☐ EMERGENCY VEHICLE
- ☐ SCHOOL BUS
- ☐ MILITARY VEHICLE
- ☐ MOTORCYCLE
- ☐ OTHER PUBLICLY OWNED VEHICLES
- ☐ MOTOR SCOOTER/BIKE
- ☐ OTHER
- ☐ TRUCK/TRUCK TRACTOR

WEATHER
(MARK ONE)

- ☐ CLEAR
- ☐ RAINING
- ☐ SNOWING
- ☒ FOG
- ☐ OTHER

ROAD SURFACE
(MARK ONE)

- ☒ DRY
- ☐ WET
- ☐ SNOWY
- ☐ ICY
- ☐ OTHER

LIGHT CONDITION
(MARK ONE)

- ☐ DAYLIGHT
- ☒ DAWN OR DUSK
- ☐ DARKNESS, LIGHTED
- ☐ DARKNESS, UNLIGHTED
- ☐ OTHER

RESIDENCE OF DRIVER NO. 1
(MARK ONE)

- ☒ LOCAL RESIDENT (WITHIN 25 MILES)
- ☐ RESIDING ELSEWHERE IN STATE
- ☐ NOT RESIDENT OF STATE

	NORTH	SOUTH	EAST	WEST
DRIVER NO. 1 WAS HEADED	☐	☒	☐	☐

ON STREET OR HIGHWAY: *De Mont*

	NORTH	SOUTH	EAST	WEST
DRIVER NO. 2 WAS HEADED	☒	☐	☒	☐

ON STREET OR HIGHWAY: *from DeMont to 14th*

DIAGRAM

NUMBER EACH VEHICLE ▷ [2] ▷ [1] ▷
USE ARROW TO SHOW PATH →
SHOW PEDESTRIAN BY ◯
RAILROAD TRACKS BY ╫╫╫╫╫╫╫╫╫╫
INDICATE DIRECTION BY ARROW AS ⊙N

S. 14th
STREET OR HIGHWAY

STREET OR HIGHWAY

De Mont
STREET OR HIGHWAY

N ↑

WERE OCCUPANTS OF VEHICLE 2 INJURED?
- ☐ YES
- ☒ NO
- ☐ DON'T KNOW

WAS THERE A POLICE OFFICER AT THE SCENE?
- ☐ YES
- ☒ NO

IF YES, WHAT DEPARTMENT?

WAS A CITATION ISSUED TO YOU?
- ☐ YES
- ☒ NO

---

1. Where was driver #1 going when the accident occurred?
2. What did driver #2 intend to do?
3. You are driver #1. Describe what happened. Get your information from the report form. This intersection is not a main one – there are no stop signs or lights – so both drivers were going slowly.
4. At 4:00 p.m. on a rainy day, you were waiting at a red light when a car pulling a small trailer hit your car from behind. Which boxes would you check if you were filling out this form?

Activities

Explain the difference between the following words:

liability insurance/personal accident
   insurance
cash/charge
deposit/refund
ticket/summons
coverage/deductible
mileage/mph

regular/unleaded/premium
mini-serve/full-serve/self-serve
fender/bumper
turn signals/tail lights/headlights
foot brake/parking brake
trunk/hood
injury/damage

Test yourself 🔲

Listen to these words and phrases from Unit 3. You may already know them, but in the conversations they have special meanings. Match them with the words on the right that mean the same. Write the letters in the blanks.

1. .... Take a left.
2. .... Big deal!
3. .... Are you kidding?
4. .... Lay off!
5. .... Fill 'er up!
6. .... Keep your shirt on!
7. .... Comin' right up!
8. .... Sure thing!
9. .... By any chance?
10. .... Never mind!

a. Leave me alone!
b. Don't be impatient!
c. Is there a possibility?
d. You'll have it very soon!
e. Don't worry, forget it!
f. Turn left.
g. Are you joking?
h. I'd like a full tank of gas.
i. Of course!
j. That's not important!

Which idioms sound friendly? Which ones sound angry? Which ones just sound polite?

GETTING AROUND

PART I

A. *Study this advertisement*

B. Read

There are three ways to get from city to city without a car. In some places, you can take Amtrak, the national passenger rail service. Or you can take a bus. Greyhound and Trailways are the largest long distance coach companies, and both of them offer monthly passes. And, of course, you can fly. There are dozens of airlines, both regional and national. Prices are not regulated, so airlines can make special offers that are sometimes cheaper than the train. There are also shuttle and commuter flights between some major cities that are close to each other.

Getting around a city on public transportation is generally not as easy as it is in most other countries, but it *is* possible. Only a few cities have subways, but most towns of 50,000 or more have some kind of city bus service.

If you can't get where you want to by bus or subway, you can always take a cab. In many cities it is almost impossible to stop a cab on the street. It's easier to call a taxi company listed in the Yellow Pages and ask them to send a cab to your door. The meter will show the amount you have to pay. The driver will usually expect a tip of at least 10%. In New York, cabs are everywhere on the streets, and cabbies expect a tip of 15%.

C. Answer the questions

1. What are this cab company's hours of operation?
2. Do the cabs have meters, or do you and the driver have to settle on a price?
3. Can you request an air-conditioned cab?
4. Does this company offer discounts on some trips?
5. If you want to have a package delivered, can you call this company?
6. Your car has a dead battery. Can you call a cab to help you get it started?
7. You work for a company that has a branch office here. Might they have an account with this cab company? If they do, what does that mean for you?
8. Does this company take credit cards? Which ones?

You can look up words on page 39.

D. Listen and answer

You will hear two conversations that take place on a city bus and in a taxi cab. Listen first and then answer the questions.

1. Who are the speakers in each conversation?
2. Where are they?
3. What's the problem in the first conversation?

4. What are the possibilities for getting around in American cities?
5. What about from city to city?

E. Listen and read 📼

This woman is at a ticket window in New York's Grand Central Station.

CLERK: Can I help you?
JILL: Yes, I'd like some information about trains to Chicago.
CLERK: Okay. What would you like to know?
JILL: Well, how many are there per day?
CLERK: One via Pittsburgh leaving at 2:45 p.m. and one via Buffalo leaving at 6:45 p.m.
JILL: How long does it take to get there?
CLERK: The Broadway – that's the one that goes through Pittsburgh – takes about eighteen hours, but the Lake Shore takes a little longer.
JILL: I see . . . What about eating and sleeping arrangements?
CLERK: Both trains have dining cars and snack bars. And there are roomettes and slumber coaches on both of them.
JILL: Well, uh, what are roomettes and slumber coaches?
CLERK: They both sleep one or two people, but the roomette has a toilet and wash basin. It costs more, too. Are you ready to make a reservation?
JILL: Uh, no, I don't think so.
CLERK: Well, here's a copy of the timetable. Why don't you take a look at it and let me know when you've decided.
JILL: Okay. Do I have to pay for the ticket when I make the reservation?
CLERK: No, you can do that later.
JILL: All right, thanks.

F. Answer and act

Listen to the conversation two or three times. The last time, take notes on what the clerk tells Jill.

1. Where does Jill want to go?
2. How many trains to that city are there each day?
3. Which train is faster?
4. Can you eat on these trains? If so, where?
5. Can you get a bed on these trains? In what kind of room?
6. Has Jill made up her mind (decided) by the end of the conversation?
7. Check your notes. Is the information you wrote correct?

GOING PLACES

Baltimore/Washington International Airport, Baltimore/Washington Parkway – Route 46, 859-7111.*

98. Greyhound Bus Station, Howard & Centre Streets. 744-9311.*

99. Penn R. R. Station, 1500 N. Charles Street. Amtrak reservations 539-2112, 1-800-523-5700 (toll-free).*

100. Trailways Bus Station, 210 W. Fayette St. 752-2115.*

👥 Read the conversation with a partner. Then one of you can read the clerk's part while the other covers the page and plays Jill. Trade roles.

PART II

A. Study this bus schedule

B. Answer the questions

1. How can you tell if a time shown on the schedule is a.m. or p.m.?
2. What are the short forms of the words "leave" and "arrive" used on this schedule?
3. What does # mean here?
4. What do MT and PT mean?
5. If you go from Salt Lake City to L.A., do you have to change buses? Where?
6. Which cities does bus 6223 run between?
7. When does 6218 leave Oakland? When does it arrive in Salt Lake City?

C. Look and listen 📼

You will hear two conversations at a bus depot. Listen to the way people offer to do something and the way other people turn them down. Looking at the bus schedule on page 34, answer the following questions.

1. You want to go from San Francisco to Salt Lake City, leaving in the morning. Where and when will your bus stop for meals?
2. How far does bus 6228 go after Salt Lake? How long does it take to get to Chicago from San Francisco?
3. The bus goes from Wells, Nevada, to Wendover, Utah, in ten minutes, but going the other direction it takes two hours and ten minutes. Can you explain this?
4. Which states do these buses go through? Find them on the map at the front of the book.

D. Problem solving 👥

Using this subway map of Boston, discuss with a friend the fastest way to get from Quincy Center to Boston College and then to Community College.

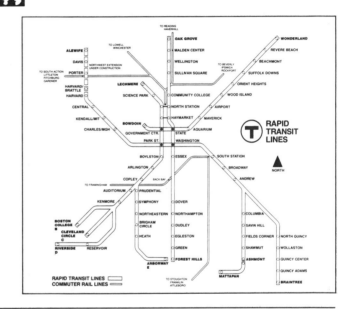

E. Turning down offers 👥

Using the following pattern and working with partners, offer to sell them a round trip ticket to Bismarck, North Dakota, to carry their suitcase up the stairs, to call a taxi for them, to help them open a window, and to read a timetable for them. Turn these offers down.

35

PART III

A. Study this sign

This is a sign you may see when you leave the international airport in New York City, JFK. See if you can understand it.

<table>
<tr><td colspan="2">taxi rates</td></tr>
<tr><td align="right">Within New York City limits</td><td>Metered rate plus tolls</td></tr>
<tr><td align="right">Newark Airport, Westchester and Nassau Counties</td><td>Doubled metered rate plus tolls</td></tr>
<tr><td align="right">All other areas</td><td>Flat rate determined by driver and passenger before departure</td></tr>
<tr><td></td><td>One fare pays for all passengers. Drivers must accept orderly fares to New York City destinations. All taxis must display the driver's name and identification number.</td></tr>
<tr><td align="right">For assistance</td><td>See taxi dispatcher, on duty
10:15 am to 2:15 am
If problems occur, contact Terminal guards or call Port Authority Police at 656-4668</td></tr>
</table>

B. Answer the questions

1. Does a taxi passenger have to pay the same amount for a trip outside New York City as inside?
2. Do additional passengers have to pay extra?
3. Who do you call if you have a problem with your taxi driver?
4. When can you get the taxi dispatcher to help you?

C. Listen and read

Here are two conversations. The first one takes place at a tourist information center in a small town near a U.S. national park. This tourist wants to go hiking in the park and needs some directions.

ATTENDANT: Hi! What can I do for you?
TOURIST: Well, I'm trying to find Rocky Mountain National Park, but I haven't seen any signs, so I'm not sure this is the right road.

ATTENDANT: It sure is. It's well marked starting on the far side of town. After that, just follow the signs. You can't miss it.
TOURIST: Thanks very much.
ATTENDANT: Sure. Have a nice day!

This man is calling a travel agency.

AGENT: Johnson's Travel. Can I help you?

HERB: Yes, I'd like some information about the special plane fares to New York I read about in your ad.

AGENT: Okay, when'll you be going and how long do you plan to stay?

HERB: Well, I'd like to leave three weeks from Friday and stay about two weeks.

AGENT: Then you qualify for our two-week advance purchase excursion fare. That's $422 if you leave Friday through Sunday, and cheaper during the week.

HERB: I guess I could leave Thursday afternoon. Are there any other restrictions?

AGENT: There's a minimum required stay of eight days.

HERB: Well, that's no problem. Can I get my ticket now?

AGENT: Sure. Come right in to our downtown office and I'll have the whole thing written up for you in a jiffy.

HERB: Okay. Can I pay with travelers checks?

AGENT: Yes. If you bring some form of identification with you, that'll be all right.

HERB: Okay, thanks. I'll be there in about an hour.

AGENT: Thank you. Bye.

Catch United's new fares... to New York!

"Hey, this is great! Thanks, Stanley."

from $392. round trip on selected flights

DEN ← I ♥ NY → JFK

for reservations (24 hour service) call 224-5000

D. *Answer the questions*

1. How can the first man get to the park?
2. What does Herb have to do to qualify for the cheaper advance purchase excursion fare? Does he qualify?

E. *Act out the scenes*

1. Read the first conversation several times with a partner. Trade roles.

2. Cover the text and tell your partner what the attendant said when she
   – greeted the hiker.
   – was asked directions to the park.

3. Read the second conversation several times with a partner. Trade roles.

4. Cover the text and tell your partner what the agent said when she
   – greeted Herb.
   – asked Herb when he'd be leaving for New York.
   – said she would have the ticket prepared.

5. Still covering the conversation, tell your partner what Herb said when he
   – asked for some information.
   – asked about restrictions.
   – asked the agent about paying for the ticket.

PART IV

A. Read

Here are some more helpful things to know.

There are several ways to pay for bus transportation in the city. In some cities, you drop your money into the fare box. In others, you have to buy tickets before you get on the bus. In some you can buy a special pass to be used for the day, week or month. And in some you buy tokens, which look something like coins, and you use them to get on the bus or enter the subway.

Subways in cities are known by different names. In Boston, the system is the MTA, sometimes called "the T." Washington, D.C., has a new subway they call the Metro, and the San Francisco Bay Area's system is BART – Bay Area Rapid Transit. In New York, it's the subway, but people often say the name of the line, e.g., the 8th Avenue. And in

Chicago, the tracks are partly underground and partly elevated, and people call the system "the el."

The Amtrak timetable is small enough to carry in your purse or pocket and contains much more than arrival and departure times. Ask for one at a travel agent's or a train station – it's free. You can charge your Amtrak tickets to a credit card.

Shuttle flights leave New York from LaGuardia Airport, and Washington from National Airport. Generally, shuttles to and from these and other cities depart once an hour from morning until 9:00 or so at night. You don't need a reservation and you can buy your ticket on board. Prices are competitive with normal commercial fares.

B. Compare

American English	British English
railroad	railway
one-way ticket	single ticket
round trip ticket	return ticket
schedule/timetable	timetable
subway	underground/Tube (London)
bus	coach/bus
downtown	town centre

GLOSSARY

ad (n): short for "advertisement"

advance (adj): earlier than usual, before

air conditioned (adj): cooled during hot weather; *air conditioning* (n): the system that cools the air in a car or building

bay (n): part of the ocean with land almost all the way around it

bold face (n): in printing, thick black letters

buck (n): a slang word for "dollar"

business account (n): a business arrangement that gives a client (or company) certain privileges, such as being billed monthly, instead of paying cash each time they buy something or use a service

cab (n): a taxi

cabbie (n): a taxi driver

coach (n): a long distance bus; *coach service* (n): a business that supplies buses

commercial (adj): existing for the purpose of making money; as advertised

commuter flight (n): a short flight, usually between a smaller town and a large city

competitive (adj): offering similar service for a similar price

connection (n): a subway, bus, train or plane planned to take passengers who change from another vehicle

contact (v): to call

depot (n): a railway or bus station

discharge (v): to let people out of a vehicle

dispatcher (n): the person at a taxi company who is in charge of the taxi drivers

downtown (n/adj): the main commercial area of a city; in New York City the words "downtown" and "uptown" mean the lower and upper sections of Manhattan Island

dozen (n): twelve

elevated (train) (n): a train that runs on a bridge above a street in a city

exception (n): something not included; something left out

excursion fare (n): a round trip fare at a reduced price

fare (n): the price charged for transportation

flat rate (n): a fixed, unchanging rate

hike (v): to travel in the country or mountains on foot; *hiker* (n): a person who hikes

jiffy (n): a moment

jumper (n): short for "jumper cables," which are electric wires from one car battery to another, used to start a car if the battery is dead

light face (n): in printing, thin letters

meter (n): a machine that shows the amount of money used or owed; *metered* (adj): on the meter

nat'l (adj): short for "national"

note (v): to point out or indicate

on duty (adv): on the job; working

operate (v): to be in action; to run; *hours of operation* (n): business hours

orderly (adj): well-behaved

pass (n): a ticket you can use as often as you want for a certain length of time

pollution (n): waste material (smoke, chemicals) that get into the air, soil or water and make them dangerous

prompt (adj): fast

purchase (n): something bought; (v): to buy

qualify (v): to fit the requirements

rapid (adj): fast

reference mark (n): a sign, letter or figure serving as a guide on a chart you look at for information

regional (adj): part of an area of the country

regulated (adj): controlled

rest stop (n): a place where a bus stops for the passengers to go to the bathroom

restriction (n): limit; limitation

roomette (n): on a train, a room with toilet and wash basin, where one or two people can sleep

round off (v): to change a number to the nearest whole number

safe (adj): not dangerous, protected

schedule (n): a timetable, list of times when something should happen

select (v): to choose; *selected* (adj): particular, certain, chosen

sidewalk (n): the surface at the side of city streets for people to walk on

slumber coach (n): on a train, a room where two people can sleep, often without toilet or wash basin

subway (n): an underground train; a system of underground railroad tracks

thru (prep): short for "through"

timetable (n): a schedule showing arrival and departure times of trains or buses

tip (n): a small amount of money given as a gift for a service; (v): to give a tip

token (n): a piece of metal used instead of a coin

trail (n): a path for people who walk or hike in the country or the mountains

transit (n): transportation

travelers checks (n): prepaid insured bank "checks" that can be used as or exchanged for cash. They are safer than cash because, if lost or stolen, they can be replaced. The word "check" may be spelled as "cheque" on travelers checks

via (prep): by way of

wash basin (n): a small sink where you can wash your hands and face

REVIEW 4

These are timetables of trains from New York to Chicago. Study them, the reference marks and Unit 4 carefully before you choose the train that best suits your needs.

New York-Boston Albany-Cleveland Toledo-Chicago — The Lake Shore Limited

READ DOWN 49					READ UP 48
Daily			Train Number		Daily
			Frequency of Operation		
Ⓡ ⌷ ✕ ⊞			Type of Service		Ⓡ ⌷ ✕ ⊞
	km	mi			
6 45 P	0	0	Dp **New York, NY** (ET) -Grand Central Terminal Ar		1 05 P
	0	0			
R 7 33 P	54	33	Dp **Croton-Harmon, NY** Ar		D 12 09 P
R 8 28 P	118	74	Poughkeepsie, NY (Highland)		D 11 22 A
8 44 P	144	89	Rhinecliff, NY (Kingston)		11 06 A
9 10 P	184	114	Hudson, NY		10 42 A
9 40 P	229	142	Ar **Albany-Rensselaer, NY** Dp		10 12 A
			Thru Cars Boston-Chicago		
449					448
Ⓡ ⌷ ⊠ ⊞			Type of Service		Ⓡ ⌷ ⊠ ⊞
4 35 P	0	0	Dp **Boston, MA** -South Sta. Ar		3 10 P
R 5 10 P	34	21	Framingham, MA •		D 2 30 P
5 45 P	71	44	Worcester, MA •		1 55 P
7 00 P	158	98	Springfield, MA •		12 40 P
8 15 P	239	149	Pittsfield, MA •		11 20 A
9 30 P	321	200	Ar **Albany-Rensselaer, NY** Dp		10 15 A
10 10 P	229	142	Dp **Albany-Rensselaer, NY** Ar		9 42 A
10 36 P	258	160	Schenectady, NY		9 09 A
11 55 P	382	238	Utica, NY		7 55 A
1 02 A	459	286	**Syracuse, NY**		7 02 A
2 28 A	597	371	**Rochester, NY**		5 17 A
3 35 A	693	431	**Buffalo, NY** -Depew Sta.		4 15 A
5 31 A	843	524	Erie, PA		2 27 A
7 12 A	995	618	Ar **Cleveland, OH** -Lakefront Sta. Dp		12 35 A
7 17 A	995	618	Ar		12 30 A
7 50 A	1036	644	Elyria, OH (Lorain)		12 00 M
8 43 A	1091	678	Sandusky, OH • ⊠		11 20 P
9 38 A	1167	725	Ar **Toledo, OH** -Central Union Tml Dp		10 15 P
353			Connecting Train Number		352
10 30 A	1167	725	Dp **Toledo, OH** (ET) Ar		9 33 P
12 20 P	1259	782	Detroit, MI -Amtrak Sta.		7 33 P
ⓔ 12 55 P	1270	789	Dearborn, MI	ⓔ	6 57 P
1 25 P	1319	819	Ann Arbor, MI		6 22 P
2 05 P	1378	857	Jackson, MI		5 42 P
3 05 P	1451	902	Battle Creek, MI		4 46 P
3 35 P	1488	924	Ar Kalamazoo, MI Dp		4 16 P
9 53 A	1167	725	Dp **Toledo, OH** -Central Union Tml Ar		10 00 P
10 50 A	1252	778	Bryan, OH • ⊠ (ET)		9 00 P
11 16 A	1382	859	Elkhart, IN (EST)		6 40 P
11 40 A	1409	876	South Bend, IN (Niles) ⬛ (EST)		6 15 P
1 35 P	1544	959	Ar **Chicago, IL** -Union Sta. (CT) Dp		4 40 P

Services

► The Lake Shore Limited
New York-Chicago; Boston-Chicago

Sleeping Car Service — Roomettes and bedrooms with complimentary coffee and tea served 6:30-9:30 AM. Also, economy slumbercoach rooms New York-Chicago.
Coach Service — Reservations required except for travel locally between New York and Albany.
Food Service — New York-Chicago—Complete meals, sandwiches, snacks and beverages; Boston-Albany — Tray meals, sandwiches, snacks and beverages.
Checked baggage — handled at all stations except Framingham, Pittsfield, Croton-Harmon, Poughkeepsie, Sandusky and Bryan.

Reference Marks

ⓔ Passengers not carried locally between Dearborn and Detroit
ⓔ Passengers not carried locally between Dearborn and Detroit except when transferring to or from VIA Rail Canada trains at Windsor.

New York-Philadelphia-Pittsburgh-Fort Wayne-Chicago

READ DOWN / READ UP

41	47		Train Number	40	46	38
The Broadway Limited	The Pennsyl-vanian		Train Name	The Broadway Limited	The Pennsyl-vanian	The Fort Pitt
Daily	Daily		Frequency of Operation	Daily	Daily	Daily
Ⓡ ⌷ ✕ ⊞	⌷		Type of Service	Ⓡ ⌷ ⊞	⌷	⌷
			(Amtrak)			
2 15 P	ⓐ 7 55 A	km 0 / mi 0	Dp **New York, NY** -Penn. Sta. (ET) Ar	4 37 P	ⓐ 10 19 P	
R 2 32 P	ⓐ 8 10 A	16 / 10	**Newark, NJ** -Penn. Sta.	D 4 20 P	ⓐ 10 00 P	
	ⓐ 8 25 A	40 / 25	Metropark, NJ -Iselin		ⓐ 9 44 P	
R 3 18 P	ⓐ 8 55 A	94 / 58	**Trenton, NJ**	D 3 35 P	ⓐ 9 13 P	
R 3 51 P	ⓐ 9 29 A	145 / 90	Ar **Philadelphia, PA** -30th St. Sta. Dp	D 3 03 P	ⓐ 8 42 P	
R 4 05 P	10 00 A	145 / 90	Dp Ar	D 2 46 P	8 10 P	
	R 10 12 A	158 / 98	Ardmore, PA ⊕			D 7 57 P
R 4 30 P	R 10 27 A	176 / 109	Paoli, PA ⊕	D 2 18 P	D 7 43 P	
ⓐ 5 16 P	11 09 A	253 / 157	Lancaster, PA	ⓐ 1 30 P	6 58 P	
ⓐ 5 55 P		310 / 192	Ar **Harrisburg, PA** (State College) ⬛ Dp	ⓐ 12 57 P	6 20 P	
ⓐ 6 05 P	11 45 A	310 / 192	Dp Ar	ⓐ 12 52 P		
7 11 P	12 55 P	408 / 254	Lewistown, PA •		11 38 A	5 05 P
7 50 P	1 35 P	467 / 290	Huntingdon, PA •		10 58 A	4 27 P
	2 02 P	499 / 310	Tyrone, PA •			4 00 P
8 33 P	2 23 P	521 / 324	Altoona, PA		10 10 A	3 37 P	8 22 P
9 37 P	3 28 P	584 / 363	Johnstown, PA		9 09 A	2 35 P	7 20 P
	4 13 P	644 / 400	Latrobe, PA •			1 52 P	6 37 P
10 31 P	4 25 P	660 / 410	Greensburg, PA •		8 13 A	1 40 P	6 25 P
		680 / 429	Pitcairn, PA •				6 06 P
11 17 P	5 05 P	710 / 441	Ar **Pittsburgh, PA** -Amtrak Sta. Dp	7 23 A	1 00 P	5 30 P
11 52 P		710 / 441	Dp Ar	6 48 A		
2 06 A		874 / 543	Canton, OH	4 23 A		
3 53 A		1014 / 630	Crestline, OH •	2 40 A		
5 20 A		1129 / 701	Lima, OH (ET)	1 02 A		
5 28 A		1225 / 761	Fort Wayne, IN (EST)	10 55 P		
ⓐ 7 40 A		1393 / 865	Valparaiso, IN • (CT)	ⓐ 8 55 P		
D 8 10 A		1423 / 884	Gary, IN • -5th & Chase Sts.	R 8 34 P		
9 00 A		1463 / 909	Ar **Chicago, IL** -Union Sta. (CT) Dp	8 00 P		

Services

► The Broadway Limited
New York-Chicago

Sleeping Cars — Roomettes and bedrooms. Complimentary coffee and tea served 6:30-9:30 AM. Also, economy slumbercoach rooms.
Reserved Coach Service.
Food Service — Dining and Lounge Service: Complete meals, sandwiches, snacks and beverages.
Checked baggage — handled at all stations except Paoli, Lancaster, Lewistown, Huntingdon, Greensburg, Canton, Crestline, Valparaiso and Gary. Only hand baggage may be checked to or from Altoona or Johnstown.

► The Pennsylvanian
Philadelphia-Pittsburgh (Amfleet)

► The Fort Pitt
Altoona-Pittsburgh (Amfleet)
Unreserved Coach Service.
Food Service — Sandwiches, snacks and beverages.
No checked baggage — passengers may carry hand baggage on board.
Note — Trains 37, 38, 39, 46 and 47 financed in part through funds made available by the Commonwealth of Pennsylvania Department of Transportation.

A—a.m.	**Km**—kilometers	**M**—midnight	**Mi**—miles	**N**—noon	**P**—p.m.
	(ET)-Eastern Time (CT)-Central Time	(MT)-Mountain Time (PT)-Pacific Time		(AT)-Atlantic Time or Alaska Time	

You want to go from New York to Chicago by train and you like to travel in style. You can't leave until 5:00 p.m. on Monday, and you have to be there by 10:30 Wednesday morning. Decide which train you'd like to take.

Activities

Find another word or words for:

cab   buck
coach   schedule
depot   rapid transit

Explain the difference between the following words and short forms:

round trip/one way   roomette/slumber coach
subway/el   a.m./p.m.
pick up/discharge   PT/MT/CT/ET

Test yourself 📼

Listen to these words and phrases from Unit 4. You may already know them, but in the conversations they have special meanings. Match them with the words on the right that mean the same. Write the letters in the blanks. (Some letters may be used more than once.)

1. .... In no time!
2. .... Here you go!
3. .... No, thank you. I'm fine.
4. .... If you say so.
5. .... You can round off to the dollar.
6. .... Where to?
7. .... That's 80 bucks even.
8. .... In a jiffy!
9. .... Getting around.
10. .... Right away!

a. In a moment!
b. That will be 80 dollars exactly.
c. Where do you want to go?
d. Traveling.
e. Here you are!
f. I don't need any help, thanks.
g. I don't agree, but it's up to you.
h. Don't count cents, only dollars.

Which idioms can you use to express that something will happen quickly? Which one could you use to turn down help politely?

PLACES TO STAY

PART I

A. Study these ads

WE ACCEPT ALL MAJOR CREDIT CARDS

MOTOR caravan HOTEL
IN THE HEART OF DOWNTOWN PORTLAND
"We Cater to Regular Commercials"
RESTAURANT & LOUNGE - BREAKFAST, LUNCH, DINNER
Direct Dial Phones—No Charge For Local Calls—Free Coffee—
Air Conditioning—Heated Pool—Individual Electric Heat—
King, Queen & Long Boy Beds—Executive Suites—
Family Units—Bridal Suite—Meeting Rooms
Color TV—Off Street Parking—Conveniently Located To Med. Hill & Vet. Hosp.
Adjacent To 12 Acre Park Jogging Track &
New YMCA Facilities
2401 S.W. 4th Avenue, Portland Or. 97201
226-1121
24 HR. DESK SERVICE

Best Western
Flamingo
BEST WESTERN MOTEL & RESTAURANT
★ 200 UNITS • MINUTES FROM AIRPORT
• 10 MIN TO DOWNTOWN
• AIRPORT LIMOUSINE • KING & QUEEN BEDS • COFFEE SHOP
• JACUZZI • SAUNA • DINING ROOM • BANQUETS 5 TO 500
• MEETING ROOMS • CONVENTION AIDS • PIANO BAR IN LOUNGE
• HEATED SWIMMING POOL • DIRECT DIAL TELEPHONES
• COMMERCIAL RATES
9727 N.E. SANDY BLVD.
255-1400

B. Read

How do you go about finding a place to stay? Well, plenty of hotels advertise at airports. If you arrive by train or car, probably the best thing to do is look in the Yellow Pages under Hotel, Motel or Lodging. You can start by comparing the services offered in their ads. In any case, you'll have to call them and see if they have the kind of room you're looking for.

Places to stay may be called hotels, motels or motor hotels, inns, lodges or resorts. These are all similar. Motels have plenty of parking space and are usually near a freeway or highway. Inns are usually like motels. Lodges and resorts, or resort hotels, are in the mountains, on the coast, or near lakes.

Beds – that's right, *beds* – also go by many different names. Starting with the smallest, there are single, twin, double, queen and king size ones. "Long boys" are for exceptionally tall people. At some hotels, queen beds are the smallest size used, so a double room has two of them. Some hotels even offer their guests waterbeds. A rollaway can be moved into a room to sleep an extra person. Hide-a-beds are sofas that fold out to make beds.

People who prefer camping to staying in hotels will have a hard time in American cities, because most of them don't have campgrounds nearby. You can camp in state and national parks, though, which generally have facilities for both tents and trailers.

C. Answer the questions

1. It's 2:00 in the morning and you want to check into a motel. Which one can you be sure is open? How can you tell?
2. You like to get some exercise in the morning. Which motel would be better for you? Why?
3. You have business downtown. Which motel will you pick and why?
4. You arrive at the airport at 10:00 p.m. and need a place to stay. Which motel will be better for you? Why?
5. One of these motels belongs to a motel chain. Which one do you think it is, and why?
6. You are going to call these two motels to see if they have a double room for three nights. Write out the questions you want to ask.

You can look up words on page 49.

D. Listen and answer 📼

You will hear two conversations. A man is calling to reserve a room in a motel. Listen first and then answer the questions.

1. Who are the people who answer the phone?
2. Where is the man calling from?
3. What kind of room does he want?
4. Does he want anything special?
5. What are the different types of places you can stay at?
6. Can you ask for various kinds and sizes of beds?
7. What about other facilities?

E. Listen and read 📼

Two people are at the reception desk of a hotel.

CLERK: Hi! Can I help you?
MARTIN: Yes, we had a reservation for this weekend.
CLERK: All right, what was the name, sir?
MARTIN: Baum, Martin Baum.
CLERK: Baum . . . Baum . . . oh, yes, here it is. A double for two nights?
MARTIN: Yes, that's right. But we were wondering . . . would you happen to have a suite available this weekend, something with a living area and a kitchenette?
CLERK: Well, the only one that's available this weekend is the executive suite, and that'll run you $140 a night.
MARTIN: I see. That's pretty high . . .
CLERK: You know, sir, this double is more than twenty feet square, and it has a refrigerator.
MARTIN: Oh, really? That sounds fine, then. What do you say, Sally?
SALLY: Sounds good to me, too.
CLERK: Good, the double then. Do you have a credit card, sir?
MARTIN: No, I'll be paying cash.
CLERK: Then I'll have to ask you to pay in advance. Fifty-five a night, plus $8 tax comes to $126. And would you fill out this registration form, please? Here's a pen. Just your name, address, and the make and license number of your car.
MARTIN: OK . . . here you are. And travelers checks for $130.
CLERK: Fine, Mr. Baum. Here's $4 change. Check-out time is 12:00 noon. The bellman will take you up . . . Harvey! Room 615 . . . If you need anything, just let me know.
MARTIN/SALLY: Thank you. Good night.

F. Answer and act

Listen to the conversation two or three times. Take notes on the information the clerk gives Martin and Sally.

1. Describe the room the Baums have gotten.
2. Is there a stove in it?
3. Why don't they rent a suite?
4. Why do they have to pay in advance?
5. What information does the clerk want from Martin?
6. When do guests have to check out of the hotel?
7. Who is going to show the Baums to their room?
8. What's their room number?
9. How does Martin pay for the room?
10. What should the Baums do if they need something?

👥 Read the conversation with a partner. Then one of you can read Martin's part while the other covers the page and plays the clerk. Trade roles.

PART II

A. Study this form

This is a laundry slip you might find in your room when you check into a hotel. Sometimes when you're traveling, you have to wash and iron your clothes, or have them laundered, and you might have to have some of them cleaned. If you want to press (or iron) your clothes yourself, you can usually get an iron from the maid. If you don't want to, take advantage of the laundry and dry cleaning service most hotels offer.

B. Answer the questions

1. What is the laundry's name?
2. Is it in the hotel?
3. Does the cleaners return clothes on the weekend?
4. Are the prices for men's and women's suits the same?
5. Where and how would you list a man's three-piece suit on this slip?
6. How much does it cost to have a three-piece suit cleaned?
7. Which prices are firm? Which ones can be higher than the price on the laundry slip?

---

10 LAUNDRY and DRY CLEANERS MAJESTIC CLEANERS

3801 N.E. Sandy Blvd. • 281-1108

Name _____

Room _____ Date_____

MON.	TUES.	WED.	THURS.	FRI.

No.	Dry Cleaning		Press Only	Amount
	Suits, Mens (2 pc)	$7.50	$5.50	
	Vests	1.75	1.25	
	Coats, Sport	4.50	3.50	
	Pants	4.00 up	3.00	
	Dresses	7.50 up	5.50	
	Evening Gowns	7.50 up	5.50	
	Suits, Lady	7.50 up	5.50	
	Skirts	4.50 up	3.50	
	Slacks, Lady	4.50 up	3.50	
	Sweaters, Shirts	4.50 up	3.50	
	Neckties	2.00 up	1.50	
	Raincoats & O'Coats	8.50 up	5.50	
	Blouses	5.00 up	3.50	
			TOTAL	

No.	Laundry	Fold	Hang		Amount
	Shirts Reg.	☐	☐	2.00	
	Shirts, Sport	☐	☐	2.25 up	
	Shirts, Knit	☐	☐	2.25	
	Pants			4.00 up	
	Handkerchiefs			.75	
	Socks, pr.			1.00	
	Undershirts			1.00	
	Undershorts			1.00	
	Pajama Pieces			2.00	
	Blouses			4.50 up	

Mark	Special Instructions	TOTAL

Surcharge on fancy or unusual items.
Prices Subject to Change Without Notice

THANK YOU

RED LION inn LLOYD CENTER®

1000 N.E. Multnomah
Portland, OR 97232
(503) 288-6111

C. Look and listen 🔲

You will hear three conversations at the Red Lion Inn. Listen to the way people ask to have things done. Then looking at the laundry slip on page 44, do the following exercises.

1. You have a man's suit, a lady's suit, a necktie and two pairs of man's pants you want to have cleaned. How would you fill out the form? Figure out how much your cleaning bill would be.
2. Make a list of the clothes you would probably take on a month-long pleasure trip or vacation. About how much would it cost to have them washed?
3. You get your cleaning back but the bill is several dollars more than you expected. You complain to the hotel clerk, and she points to a line on the laundry form which explains the price increase. Find the line.
4. You have a cotton shirt from India that will fade and shrink if it is machine washed, or pressed with steam. Write some special instructions for the cleaners.

D. Problem solving 👥

You have decided to hold a convention at the *Holiday Inn* in Dodge City. Call them to ask some questions about facilities and get reservations for 50 people for next month. Give the clerk the exact dates you need the convention center for and spell the names of the contact people.

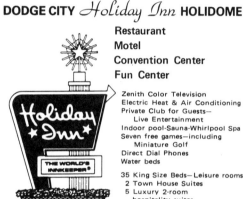

DODGE CITY *Holiday Inn* **HOLIDOME**

Restaurant
Motel
Convention Center
Fun Center

Zenith Color Television
Electric Heat & Air Conditioning
Private Club for Guests—
    Live Entertainment
Indoor pool-Sauna-Whirlpool Spa
Seven free games—including
    Miniature Golf
Direct Dial Phones
Water beds

35 King Size Beds—Leisure rooms
 2 Town House Suites
 5 Luxury 2-room
    hospitality suites
 2 Handicap rooms
65 2 bed Holiday rooms
TOTAL 109 Rooms

HOLIDOME—16000 sq. ft. of enclosed temperature controlled space for exhibits and display.

CONVENTION CENTER—5000 sq. ft. that can be divided into 6 rooms. Made to accomodate several hundred people.

Call *Holiday Inn* Reservation Center
800-238-8000

Dodge City *Holiday Inn* Holidome
316-225-9900

E. Having things done 👥

Using the following pattern and working with a partner, ask someone at the hotel to have your laundry done, to have a blouse or shirt ironed, to have your car looked at or repaired, to have a rollaway bed moved into your room, to have a meeting room scheduled, to have a long distance call to Buffalo, N.Y., dialed by the hotel switchboard operator and to have a table reserved for dinner. The hotel employees should assure their partners that it will be done immediately.

Say hello.

Give positive reply.

HOTEL RECEPTION

Respond and ask to have something done.

Thank.

PART III

A. Study this questionnaire

You may see something like this in a hotel or resort where you are staying. See if you can understand it.

How well are we serving you?

To us your comfort and satisfaction are all-important.

We kindly ask that you take a moment to respond to our hospitality "report card." Your opinions will assist us in maintaining the quality of service that travelers have come to expect from Amfac Hotels and Restaurants.

We know we have to earn your patronage, and that's what we intend to do. Your happiness is our business.

Amfac Hotels and Restaurants

Your room # _____

Reservations

How was your reservation made?

Check One

Directly to this hotel
Through our toll free reservation number
By a travel agent

Was your reservation handled courteously?   Yes   No
Was your reservation in order at check-in?

Reception and Service

How would you rate the courteousness, promptness and efficiency of the following:

Excellent / Good / Satisfactory / Poor

Driver
Bellperson
Desk Clerk
Telephone Operator
Cashier at Checkout

Guest Rooms

How would you rate your guest room on the following:

Excellent / Good / Satisfactory / Poor

Cleanliness
Comfort
Working condition (TV, lighting, etc.)
Supplied properly (towels, soap, etc.)

If you made maintenance requests were they met promptly?   Yes   No

Lounges

How would you rate our lounge on the following?

Excellent / Good / Satisfactory / Poor

Prompt Service
Courtesy of waiter or waitress

General

How do you rate our overall hotel service and facilities?

Excellent / Good / Satisfactory / Poor

Have you been our guest before?   Yes   No
Would you return to this hotel?

How did you hear about us?

Check One

Advertising
Friend or Relative
Travel Agent

If you met an outstanding employee, please let us know his/her name _____
Have you any remarks that may help to improve our service? _____

(Optional)

Name _____
Address _____
City _____   State _____   Zip _____
Date _____

Please seal and return to front desk or mail

DFW

B. Answer the questions

1. Why are they asking you to fill out this questionnaire?
2. What should you do with it after you've filled it out?
3. If you've stayed in a hotel recently, try to fill out the form.

C. Listen and read 📼

Here are two conversations that might take place at a hotel or motel. In the first one, a man is calling the front desk from his room because there are a couple of things wrong.

CLERK: Front desk.

MARTIN: Hello. This is Martin Baum. The bathroom light in my room doesn't work. Could you have somebody come up and take a look at it, please?

CLERK: Oh, of course, Mr. Baum. What room number was that, please?

MARTIN: Room 615.

CLERK: Okay, I'll have a man up there in a minute.

MARTIN: Fine. And another thing – I don't seem to have a room service menu. Is there one?

CLERK: Yes, there is. We have 24-hour room service. I'm sorry about that. I'll have a room service waiter bring you a menu up right away.

MARTIN: Thanks.

CLERK: If you need anything else, just let me know.

MARTIN: I will. Good night.

CLERK: Good night.

The second conversation takes place in a hotel lobby at the hotel reception desk, where two people have just registered.

CLERK: All right. The bellman will take your bags up for you.

BILL: Oh, we'd like to do some shopping this afternoon. Could you give us some advice on where the best place to go might be?

CLERK: Sure. There's a gift shop here in the hotel, and a tobacco shop, and we're in the business district, so you can reach the city's best stores on foot. Did you want to shop for clothing or what?

KATHY: Yes, we'd like to shop for both men's and women's clothes and shoes, and maybe cookware, too.

CLERK: All right, when you leave the hotel, turn left. You'll be heading south. Two blocks down the street is a very nice department store called Nordstrom's. Three blocks farther there are two shoe stores, and one block east there is a cookware shop called Kitchen Kaboodle.

BILL: I'd also be interested in a bookstore, and a game or toy store.

CLERK: Hmm . . . there's a bookstore at the corner of 8th and Silver Streets – that's west of Nordstrom's. I'm not sure if they carry games or not. And there's an import shop up the street a block from there. They might carry kitchen stuff, too. And then you can always go out to Beaverton Mall. That's a shopping center about five miles away.

BILL: Okay, thanks a lot.

D. Answer the questions

1. What things did the first guest ask the hotel clerk to have done for him?
2. What advice do the guests in the second conversation ask the clerk for?
3. What stores does she tell them about and what else does she suggest?

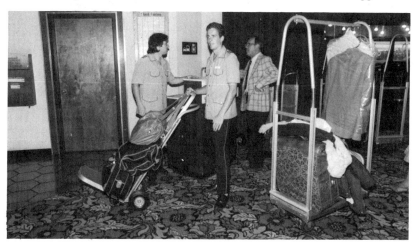

E. Act out the scenes

1. Read the first conversation several times with a partner. Trade roles.

2. Cover the conversations. Then tell your partner exactly what Martin said when he
   – complained about the bathroom light.
   – asked the clerk to have someone look at the light.
   – said he didn't have a room service menu.

3. With a partner, read the second conversation several times. Trade roles.

4. Cover the conversation and tell your partner exactly
   – how Bill asked for advice on where to go shopping.
   – how Kathy described what they would like to shop for.
   – how Bill said he would be interested in a bookstore.

5. Listen to the second conversation again and take notes on where the stores are.

PART IV

I think we ought to tip the maid in advance!

A. Read

Here are some more helpful things to know.

Who should you tip at a hotel? The bellman gets 50¢ to $1 per bag for taking your luggage to your room. Maids usually don't expect a tip, but if you stay more than a few days or if your maid does something special for you, a $2 tip is a good idea. Room service waiters should get 15% of a bill.

You may want to avoid some motels that advertise "in-room movies" or "in-house films." These are usually X-rated, or pornographic, films.

Lots of hotels have special facilities for conventions – large and small meeting rooms, banquet rooms, PA (public address) systems and so on. They may also offer guests attending the convention special rates on services.

Electricity in North America is 110 volts (60 Herz) – not 220. This means you won't

be able to use your hair dryer or your electric razor unless you can change it to 110 volts.

When telephoning from your hotel room, you will often have to go through the hotel switchboard, especially for long distance calls. These calls can be quite expensive, because the hotel usually adds a high service charge to the calls you make. On the other hand, local calls can generally be made from your room by dialing direct. You can also ask the hotel receptionist to give you a wake up call in the morning.

If your hotel does not have a laundry service, maybe you can find a laundromat nearby, which might even be open 24 hours a day. You will need exact change to operate the washing machines and dryers.

You will always find soap, towels and linen in hotel and motel rooms in the U.S.

B. Compare

American English	British English
lobby	foyer
front desk	reception
desk clerk	receptionist
elevator	lift
first floor	ground floor
second floor	first floor
stove	cooker
vest	waistcoat
pants	trousers
undershirt	vest
undershorts/underwear	pants

GLOSSARY

accommodate (v): to give someone a room in which to live or stay

advice (n): opinion given by one person to another on how to do something

assure (v): say positively

attract (v): to catch someone's attention and make them want to come near

banquet (n): a large meal served to a lot of people, often at a convention

bellman (n): in a hotel, the person who carries luggage to the room

bridal suite (n): an expensive suite in a hotel for newly married couples

business district (n): the area of a town where you shop and work

cashier (n): a person who takes money in a hotel, store, etc.

cater to (v): to give customers what is necessary, to serve

chain (n): a number of shops, hotels, restaurants, etc., owned by the same person or company

cleaning or dry cleaning (n): a method of cleaning clothes with chemicals

closet (n): a very small room to keep clothes and other things in

commercial rates (n): special rates for business travelers

contact (n): a person you plan to meet or have met to do business with

convenient (adj): suited to your needs

convention (n): a meeting of a large number of people to take action about a common interest; also, the annual business meeting of an organization with many branches in different areas

cookware (n): containers used for cooking

courteousness (n): the act of being polite and kind and showing good manners

dryer (n): a machine for drying clothes with hot air

efficiency (n): the ability to do things well without wasting time, energy or money

executive suite (n): an expensive suite in a hotel for traveling business people

exercise (n): activity for training and developing the body

exhibit (n): a public show or display

expense account (n): a fund of money for paying business expenses while traveling or while entertaining business guests

facilities (n): equipment

fade (v): to lose the original color

freeway (n): a large highway

handicap (n): a disability; *handicapped* (adj): having a disadvantage or disability of body or mind

head (v): to move in a certain direction

hospitality (n): welcoming behavior to guests

ignore (v): to pay no attention to

iron (v): to press clothes with a heated, heavy object to make them smooth and dry

Jacuzzi (n): a brand name water massage machine for the bath tub

kitchenette (n): a small kitchen

knit (adj): made by knitting, using two large needles and yarn, e.g., wool sweaters

laundromat (n): a place with coin-operated washing machines

laundry (n): clothes that need to be washed; also, a business that washes clothes

linen (n): sheets and pillowcases for your bed

lobby (n): area of a hotel where the reception desk is located

lodging (n): a place to stay for a short time

lounge (n): a comfortable room, often in an airport, hotel, etc., where people sit and talk, or wait; often, the bar in such a place

maintain (v): keep; *maintenance* (n): the department of a building that keeps everything in good repair

notice (n): a sign informing people about something

o'coat (n): short for "overcoat," a heavy coat men wear over their suits

outstanding (adj): very good

overall (adj/adv): general, including everything

patronage (n): the use of a service by customers

public address system (n): microphones and loudspeakers used by speakers to large groups of people; also, *PA system*

rate (v): to set a value on

resort (n): a place people go to relax and have fun, usually for a vacation

rollaway bed (n): a bed that folds up and can be put in a closet or moved into a room

schedule (v): to plan for a certain time

service charge (n): the price for service, e.g., a 10% service charge added to the bill

shrink (v): to get smaller

sleep (v): to have room for people to sleep

slip (n): a small piece of paper

spa (n): a health resort

square (adj): the size of an area as measured by length and width together

stuff (n): things

suite (n): in a hotel, a group of rooms, bedroom, bathroom, living area and kitchen

sweater (n): a warm knitted piece of clothing for the upper body

switchboard (n): the central control for the telephone lines in a building

undershirt (n): knit shirts men wear under their shirts

undershorts (n): short pants men wear under their pants

unit (n): a room or suite in a motel

vacancy (n): at a hotel, an empty room

vest (n): a piece of clothing with no sleeves to wear over a shirt or blouse

wake up call (n): a quick phone call from your hotel receptionist to wake you in the morning

whirlpool (n): a machine that circulates water in the bath tub or swimming pool

X-rated (adj): for adults only; pornographic

REVIEW 5

This ad uses "flowery" language to describe the features of a new hotel in Atlanta, Georgia. Read the ad to get the general meaning and the main message and ignore the unnecessary descriptive words. Read the ad and then answer the questions below. If you can answer them, you've done a good job of getting the message!

Hartley Inn

HARTLEY HOTELS AND MOTOR INNS
A worldwide chain of excellence

1. What is the hotel's name?
2. Is it an independent or a chain hotel? Who owns it?
3. How many units (rooms and suites) does the hotel have?
4. How many eating places does the hotel have? Which one sounds more expensive? More casual?
5. Does the hotel have facilities for guests to use in their free time?
6. Does the hotel have facilities for business meetings and conventions? What are they?
7. Are there any shopping facilities in the hotel? What are they?
8. What special transportation services does the hotel provide?
9. Does this hotel try harder to attract business people or tourists? What makes you think so?
10. Does it have special facilities for men or women? What are they? Do you think more men or women stay at this hotel? Why?

Innovative interior design and decorative motif sparked with a sophisticated international flavor

200 colorfully-decorated guest rooms and suites

The Polo Restaurant, with its plush appointments and select international cuisine

The Polo Lounge, featuring an intimate setting and entertainment nightly

The Scandia Cafe — cheery, casual and charmingly continental coffee shop

4,700 square feet of modern meeting, banquet and convention space

The Games — billiards room with a cozy, masculine decor / United Press International (UPI) news machine

Full-facility Decathlon Health Club for men

Lighted tennis and handball courts jogging track / putting green

Free-form, tunnel-connected, heated swimming pool surrounded by a spacious patio — Victory Court. Colorful cabana bar and putting green adjacent to pool

Eastern Airlines ticket desk in lobby

Gift and barber shops

Airport limousines / auto rental and repair valet / room service

Free local telephone calls

Activities

These people work at hotels. What do they do?

desk clerk   maid
switchboard operator bellman
room service waiter

These are typical rooms in hotels. Why do people go there and what is special about each place?

front desk meeting room
lobby   game room
lounge   gift shop
suite   piano bar

Test yourself 📼

Listen to these words and phrases from Unit 5. You may already know them, but in the conversations they have special meanings. Match them with the words on the right that mean the same. Write the letters in the blanks. (Some letters may be used more than once.)

1. .... It doesn't work.
2. .... They happen to have some.
3. .... That'll run you $140.
4. .... Could you see to that?
5. .... Something's wrong with it.
6. .... You'll be heading south.
7. .... I'll have a man there.
8. .... That store carries it.
9. .... Take advantage of it.
10. .... Could I have that done?

a. I will send someone.
b. Could you get someone to do that for me?
c. Something isn't right.
d. You will be going south.
e. Make use of it.
f. That will cost 140 dollars.
g. They have some by chance.
h. It is broken.
i. Could you do that?
j. The store has it for sale.

Which idioms express that something is broken and which ones would you use to ask someone to repair it?

HANDLING YOUR MONEY

PART I

A. Study these ads

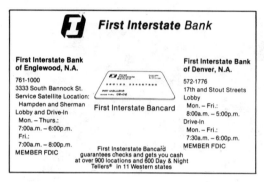

First Interstate Bank

First Interstate Bank of Englewood, N.A.

761-1000
3333 South Bannock St.
Service Satellite Location:
Hampden and Sherman
Lobby and Drive-In
Mon. – Thurs.:
7:00a.m. – 6:00p.m.
Fri.:
7:00a.m. – 8:00p.m.
MEMBER FDIC

First Interstate Bancard

First Interstate Bank of Denver, N.A.

572-1776
17th and Stout Streets
Lobby
Mon. – Fri.:
8:00a.m. – 5:00p.m.
Drive-In
Mon. – Fri.:
7:30a.m. – 6:00p.m.
MEMBER FDIC

First Interstate Bancard guarantees checks and gets you cash at over 900 locations and 600 Day & Night Tellers® in 11 Western states

Western Bank

Throughout the State . . .

MERCER HEAD OFFICE:
4127 W JEFFERSON BLVD
072-1000

WEST PARK BRANCH
211 W HARVEY
489-0347

GLENDALE BEACH BRANCH
23 OCEAN SHOPPING MALL
300-3000

EAST LODGE BRANCH
2073 CULVER BLVD
830-4444

DRIVE UP AND WALK UP WINDOW SERVICE
EXTENDED BANKING HOURS:

- Checking Accounts
- Savings Accounts
- Certificates of Deposits
- Safe Deposit Boxes
- Escrow Department
- Automobile Loans
- Installment Loans
- Business Loans
- Home Improvement Loans
- Night Depository Service
- Banclub Acct
- Collection Cheques
- Travelers Cheques
- Bank by Mail – Merchants Visa

B. Read

Most banks in the U.S. open at 9:00 or 10:00 and close between 3:00 and 5:00, but stay open later on Fridays. Some banks have longer hours in order to attract customers. These are ads like those you would find in the Yellow Pages under Banks.

What's the best way to carry money safely while you're traveling? There are three possibilities – personal checks from your country, travelers checks and credit cards. Some American banks accept foreign checks such as Eurocheques; the problem is that only those banks that are used to dealing with foreigners will know what Eurocheques are.

It may be more convenient to carry travelers checks, which are insured against loss. They should be in dollars, because only a few banks do much business in foreign currencies. If your checks aren't in dollars, it may take you a long time to find a bank that will exchange them. You can use travelers checks almost anywhere – in restaurants, stores or ticket offices – without having to go to a bank. If you run out of them, you can buy more at most banks. Their service charge will vary, though, so ask what it is before you buy your checks.

Americans would say the best way to carry money is to have a major credit card like Visa, MasterCard or American Express. Credit cards can be canceled if they are lost or stolen. And because they are widely accepted in the U.S., it is easy to use them to pay for lodging, transportation, meals and things you want to buy from larger stores.

Of course you can't get along without cash, but you don't need to carry much with you.

C. Answer the questions

1. Do you think Western Bank has longer or shorter hours than most banks? Why?
2. What are First Interstate Bank's hours? Are they unusual?
3. How many branches does Western have?
4. Which bank sells travelers checks?
5. Which bank has connections in other states?
6. Is it a good idea to have a credit card when you travel in the U.S.? What kind?
7. What is the best way to carry cash?
8. What currency should travelers checks be in? Is it convenient to carry them in Swiss francs? Why or why not?
9. Where should you go if you want to cash a Eurocheque?
10. Can you buy travelers checks at banks?

You can look up words on page 59.

D. Listen and answer 📼

You will hear a conversation at a bank. Listen first and then answer the questions.

1. Who are the speakers?
2. What does the man want?
3. How does he want to pay?
4. What do you have to show the teller at an American bank if you want to pay with foreign checks?
5. What do you do if you lose your travelers checks?

E. Listen and read 📼

This man lost his travelers checks yesterday. Now he's just come back from the travelers check office.

JOYCE: Did you get your checks replaced?
PAUL: Yes, but it was complicated. I went to the office downtown and they told me I had to call New York before they could do anything. So they let me use their phone – it was a toll-free number. The woman asked me how much I'd lost and what the check numbers were. Thank God I had them written down.
JOYCE: Well, that doesn't sound so bad.
PAUL: But it's not the whole story. She wanted to know where I bought the checks and if I had any ID. I gave her my passport number. Then she gave me a "file number" and told me where the nearest refund office was. I told her I was already there. Then she wanted to talk to the agent. After they hung up, I had to fill out a form with all the same information on it. Then finally the agent okayed the thing, after her supervisor had initialed it, and I got my checks.
JOYCE: Well, at least it didn't cost you anything.
PAUL: You're right, and if I hadn't had the numbers, it could've been a lot more complicated.

F. Answer and act

Listen to the conversation two or three times. Then try to answer the questions without looking at the conversation.

1. What happened to Paul yesterday?
2. What did he want the travelers check company to do when he went to their office?
3. What did he have to do first?
4. Did he have to pay for the phone call? Why or why not?
5. What were four things the woman in New York wanted to know?
6. Why was it fairly easy for Paul to get new checks? What would have made it more difficult?

Pretend you are filling out this lost travelers check form for your partner. Ask him or her questions like this: "What's your name?" Trade roles.

1. Name
2. Address
3. Date, location and circumstances of loss
4. Documents of identification lost
5. Currency of checks
6. Amount of loss
7. The lost travelers checks were:
   Check one: ☐ Signed by me only in the upper right corner
   ☐ Signed by me in the upper right corner and countersigned by me in the lower left corner
   ☐ Neither signed nor countersigned by me in the upper right or lower left corner
8. Date of purchase
9. Amount of purchase

PART II

A. Study this form

The telegraph company will have one like this for you to fill out when you need to wire money to someone.

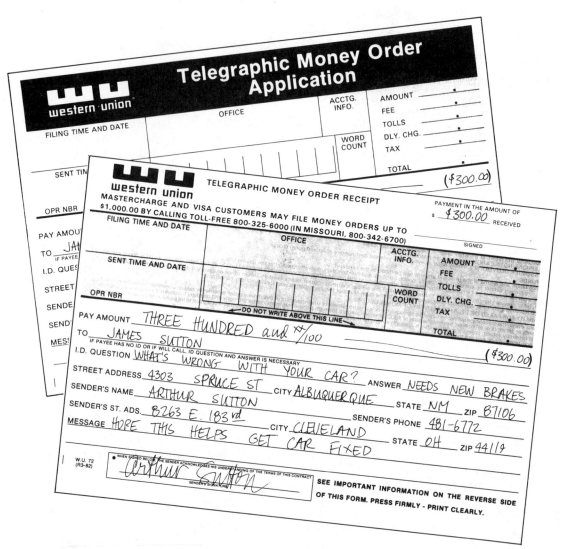

B. Answer the questions

1. Who's sending the telegram?
2. What's his address and phone number?
3. What's the recipient's name?
4. What's his address and phone number?
5. How much money is being cabled to him?
6. What's Arthur's message to James?
7. What question does James have to answer in order to get the $300?
8. What's on the back of this form?
9. How can you send a money order if you have a Visa or MasterCard?
10. How much money can you send this way?

C. *Look and listen* 📼

You will hear three conversations in the telegraph office. Listen to the way people ask how long it will take to do things. Looking at the forms on pages 54 and 16, write the following messages.

1. You are nineteen and on vacation alone. You run out of money. Write a telegram to your parents for help.

2. You want to wire money to your daughter in India, using your Visa card. Fill out the form and phone as much money to her as possible.

3. You are in Houston for a meeting that will last longer than expected. Write a telegram to your boss in Boston saying you'll be late and can't meet a deadline.

D. *Problem solving* 👥

1. You have been waiting for an appliance you ordered from ABC Electrical to be sent C.O.D. (cash on delivery). The delivery person brings it to your door, you pay for it and then he shows you where to sign the receipt. After that he signs and dates it himself.
2. Explain to someone the differences between banking, postal and telegraph services in your country and in the U.S.

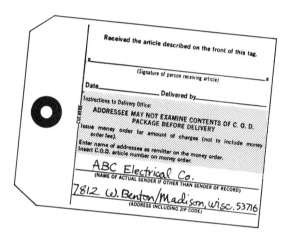

E. *Asking and telling how long* 👥

Using the following pattern and working with a partner, ask and tell someone how long it will take to send a telegram to your country, to get money from Japan, to replace your lost travelers checks, to wire $1,000 to Alaska, to get to Dayton, Ohio, by train and to get downtown and to the airport.

PART III

A. Study this form

This is a credit application form from a large department store. See if you can understand it.

MISS ☐ MRS. ☐ MR. ☐	FIRST NAME	INITIAL	LAST NAME		Husband's or Wife's Name	Widow ☐ Divorced ☐ Separated ☐

PRESENT ADDRESS	HOW LONG

	CITY	STATE	ZIP CODE	PHONE NUMBER

FORMER ADDRESS	AGE

NUMBER OF DEPENDENTS INCLUDE SELF AS ONE	RESIDENCE (CHECK ONE) OWN ☐ RENT ☐ ROOM ☐ LIVE WITH PARENTS ☐

EMPLOYMENT

	HUSBAND OR SINGLE PERSON	EMPLOYED BY	POSITION & BADGE NO.	SALARY
		ADDRESS	BUSINESS PHONE	HOW LONG
	WIFE	EMPLOYED BY	POSITION & BADGE NO.	SALARY
		ADDRESS	BUSINESS PHONE	HOW LONG
	FORMER EMPLOYER SELF ☐ SPOUSE ☐		POSITION	HOW LONG

BANK	BRANCH OR ADDRESS	Savings ☐ Reg. Check ☐ Spec. Check ☐

PLEASE LIST FIRMS THAT HAVE GIVEN YOU CREDIT

FIRM NAME	ADDRESS	Account Number
1		
2		

PERSONAL REFERENCE	ADDRESS	PHONE NUMBER

AUTHORIZED BUYER	RELATIONSHIP	YOUR SOCIAL SECURITY NUMBER

RETAIL INSTALLMENT CREDIT AGREEMENT

I may, within 25 days of the closing date appearing on the periodic statement of my account, pay in full the "new balance" appearing on said statement and thereby avoid a FINANCE CHARGE; or, if I so choose, I may pay my account in monthly installments in accordance with the schedule below. If I avail myself of the latter option, I will incur and pay a FINANCE CHARGE computed at a periodic rate of 1½% per month (an ANNUAL PERCENTAGE RATE of 18%) on that portion of the previous balance which does not exceed $500.00 (subject to a minimum charge of 50¢) and 1% per month (an ANNUAL PERCENTAGE RATE of 12%) on that portion of said balance which exceeds $500.00. For convenience, however, there will be no FINANCE CHARGE on balances of $5.00 or less. The FINANCE CHARGE will be computed on the previous balance without deducting any payments or other credits and without adding current purchases.

Notice to the buyer: 1. Do not sign this credit agreement before you read it or if it contains any blank space. 2. You are entitled to a completely filled in copy of this credit agreement at the time you sign it. 3. You may at any time pay your total indebtedness hereunder. 4. Keep this agreement to protect your legal rights.

PAYMENT SCHEDULE	If Indebtedness is	$ .01 to 10.00	$10.01 to 60.00	$60.01 to 90.00	$ 90.01 to 120.00	$120.01 to 180.00	$180.01 to 240.00	Over $240.00
	Monthly Payment is	Full Balance	$10.00	$15.00	$20.00	$30.00	$40.00	1/5 of Balance

APPROVED BY:_____	BUYER'S SIGNATURE:_____

B. Answer the questions

1. Why are they asking you to fill out this form?
2. What information is required for the application to be processed?
3. Why do you have to list your employer, former employer, former credit references and personal references?
4. Try to fill out the application.

C. Listen and read 📼

Here are two conversations that might take place in a large department store. The first customer is choosing and paying for some things she wants to buy.

CLERK: May I help you find something?

ALICE: No, thanks, I'm just looking. Uh, well, maybe you can. I'd like to buy a nice pair of jeans and one of these tailored jackets for my husband's birthday, but I'm not sure which of the jackets he'd like best.

CLERK: Mmm-hmm. This one is cut very nicely and it's very popular right now.

ALICE: Yes, I like it, too. And the color would look good on him. But I just don't know . . .

CLERK: You might consider getting him a gift certificate, you know. Then he could come in and get exactly what he wants and then it would be sure to fit.

ALICE: Yes, that *is* an idea . . . but . . . uh, would he be able to exchange the jacket if I got him one today and he didn't like it?

CLERK: Yes, of course, within thirty days as long as he has the receipt.

ALICE: Then I guess I'll take this one.

CLERK: Fine. I'll write it up over here . . . uh, do you have a credit card, ma'am?

ALICE: Yes, I do.

CLERK: Okay, just take this sales slip and your card over to register 12 and the cashier'll ring it up for you.

CASHIER: Here you go. Just sign the slip here, please, and here's your bag.

The second customer wants to buy an electric heater.

CLERK: How do you like it?

MARK: Great. I'll take it. But first I want to know how long the guarantee is for.

CLERK: One year. Here's the warranty. See?

MARK: Uh-huh. Fine.

CLERK: Will that be cash or charge?

MARK: Cash. But I'm afraid there's a problem. I'm from Oklahoma. You won't take an out-of-state check, will you?

CLERK: No, I'm afraid not.

MARK: I didn't think so. Uh . . . my girlfriend has our travelers checks. I'm meeting her in half an hour, so I'd like to ask you to hold this heater till I can get back.

CLERK: Oh, no problem, sir. What's the name?

MARK: Parodi.

CLERK: Okay, Mr. Parodi. It'll be right here. The cashier'll take care of you when you bring your travelers checks.

MARK: Thanks a lot.

CLERK: You bet.

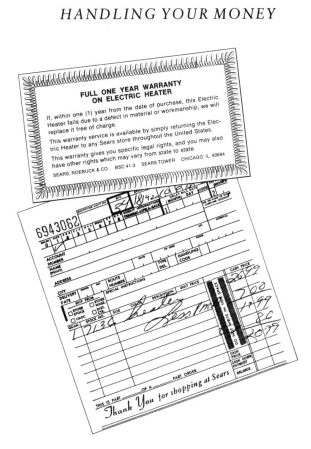

D. Answer the questions

1. If the first customer wants to exchange anything, how long does she have and what does she have to keep?
2. What did Mark want to know before deciding on the heater?
3. What was the problem?
4. Will they hold the heater for him?

E. Act out the scenes

1. Read the first conversation several times with a partner. Trade roles.

2. Cover the text and say exactly
   – how the clerk greeted Alice.
   —how Alice first said she didn't need help and then changed her mind.
   —how they talked about the jacket and how it would fit and look on Alice's husband.
   —how the clerk suggested a gift certificate instead of the jacket.
   —how Alice asked about exchanging the jacket.
   —what the clerk said about the store's policy on that.
   —how the clerk told Alice to pay.

3. Decide if the clerk is being casual, polite or formal. If he were being more casual, what do you think he would say to Alice?

4. With your partner, read the second conversation aloud a few times. Trade roles.

5. Cover the text and say Mark's exact words when he
   – asked about a guarantee.
   – told the clerk there was a problem.
   – asked the clerk to hold the heater for him.

PART IV

A. Read

Here are some more helpful things to know.

American money comes in coins worth 1¢ (pennies), 5¢ (nickels), 10¢ (dimes), 25¢ (quarters) and 50¢, though half dollars aren't very common. Paper money is in denominations of $1, $5, $10 and $20. Two, fifty and one-hundred dollar bills exist, but they aren't common. Don't be surprised if a bank teller or store clerk looks very closely at a hundred dollar bill to make sure it's real!

Travelers checks are insured. If they are lost or stolen, you will get your money back – the only question is when. Keep a record of your checks separate from the checks themselves.

When you pay for something with your credit card, the salesperson will take your card and fill out a form using a computer or a machine. He or she will ask you to sign the form and then give you a copy. The credit card company sends you a bill once a month that shows the purchases you made and any balance left to pay from the month before. Usually you have thirty days to pay before they charge you interest. Check with your company to find out details about the interest they charge.

The word "national" in the name of many banks does not mean they have branches everywhere in the country; in fact, banks are not allowed to have branches in more than one state. Laws about banks are made by each state. In some states, banks are not allowed to have branches at all. Even in states where they are allowed, there may not be many branches of any one bank.

If you write a personal check and it bounces, you will have to pay the bank a high service charge on it. So be sure you always have enough money in your account to cover any checks you write.

Layaway is a service offered by many stores selling items that cost up to $300. The customer pays 10%–50% of the price and agrees to pay the rest by a certain date, usually not more than thirty days later. The store keeps the item until the customer pays the whole price. Customers who don't return to pay for the item before that date lose their money, but otherwise there is no charge.

Many stores that sell expensive items – home appliances like washing machines and refrigerators, for example – allow their customers to pay for them on the installment plan. Customers make a down payment of 10% or more on the purchase price and pay the rest in monthly installments. They also have to pay interest.

B. Compare

American English	British English
bank teller	cashier
(dollar) bill	(pound) note
checking account	current account
installment plan	hire purchase/instalment
to exchange	to change
to wire	to telegram

GLOSSARY

account (n): money kept in the bank that can be added to or taken from

addressee (n): a person to whom something is sent

appliance (n): an instrument or machine, especially for household use

apply (v): to ask for something officially in writing, e.g., apply for credit

balance (n): the amount of money remaining

bill (n): paper money

branch (n): an office of a bank, store, etc., that is not the main office

bounce (v): (of a check) to be returned by a bank as worthless

cable (v): to send a telegram

cancel (v): to make invalid

cash (v): to exchange a check (or other order to pay) for cash

circumstances (n): the state of affairs

C.O.D. (n): cash on delivery, you pay when something is brought to your door

complicated (adj): not simple

consumer (n): a person who buys things

convert (v): to change into something else

countersign (v): to sign a second time in order to make the first signature or the paper being signed valid

cover (v): to pay for

cut (adj): made, designed

deadline (n): the time when something has to be finished

denomination (n): a unit or group, e.g., American money has denominations of $1, $5, etc.

depend (v): to be different according to circumstances, e.g., depend on something

draw on (v): to make use of money

exchange rate (n): the value of money of one country or the cost of buying currency from another country

file number (n): an official number recorded when information is being collected on a person

finance charge (n): interest

garment (n): a piece of clothing

gift certificate (n): a coupon that can be bought at many stores and exchanged later for merchandise; you can get a gift certificate for someone when you don't know what present to give

guarantee (n): a product certificate that is an agreement to replace or repair the product if it is necessary

hold (v): to keep for someone

initial (v): to write your initials

installment (n): a regularly scheduled payment of a debt

interest (n): money paid for the use of money

landlord (n): the person who owns or rents out an apartment or building, or the owner's agent who is responsible for taking care of problems

layaway (n): an agreement that a store will hold a particular item and the customer's small first payment until he can pay the full price

major (adj): important

merchandise (n): the things that a store has for sale

money order (n): a check, or order for payment; it is often necessary to buy a money order when you do not have a personal checking account and want to pay for something through the mail, or when a company will not accept personal checks. Money orders are available at banks or post offices

night letter (n): a telegram that is sent during the night and delivered the next day; it costs less to send than a regular telegram

okay (v): to approve

personal reference (n): a person who can give favorable information about your character; or a written statement with such information

policy (n): the rules followed in making decisions

previous (adj): earlier

process (v): to carry out the required steps in order to make a decision about and complete action on something

purchase (n): something that has been bought, or purchased

refund (v): to give back a customer's money when he returns merchandise that he is not satisfied with for some reason, e.g., bad quality, wrong size, etc.

register or *cash register* (n): a machine in a store used for adding prices and keeping money

remitter (n): a person sending money

replace (v): to put something back or exchange something for full value

sales slip (n): a receipt given in a shop

service charge (n): a charge in addition to the cost of an item

supervisor (n): a person in charge of others; a boss

tailored (adj): made by cutting and sewing to a person's measurements; often used to mean well-cut, or having the look of being tailored

teller (n): a person who works at the counter in a bank

terms (n): the conditions of an agreement

unaltered (adj): unchanged

upper limit (n): the largest amount permitted

vary (v): to differ

wallet (n): a small purse that holds paper money and fits in your pocket

warranty (n): a guarantee

wire (v): to send a telegram

REVIEW 6

These are forms like those you would see if you wanted to open a checking account in an American bank. Savings account forms are different. Study them and Unit 6 carefully before you answer the questions below.

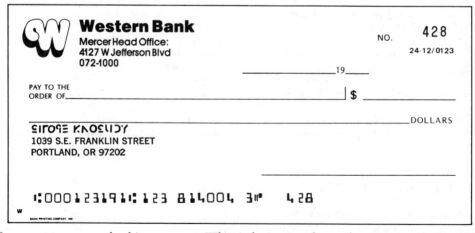

I, We, hereby agree to the By-Laws of WESTERN BANK and all amendments thereto.

CHECK ONE FOR IRS DIVIDEND REPORT

Social Security No.

Signature

Individual ☐   Joint ☐   Trust ☐   Other ☐   Social Security No.

Signature

Your Home Address

Zip Code   Zip Code

Father's Name

Mother's Name

Name of Spouse

Occupation   Your Birthdate   Occupation

Western Bank
Mercer Head Office:
4127 W Jefferson Blvd
072-1000

DATE

SIGN HERE IN PRESENCE OF TELLER FOR CASH RET'D FROM DEP.
X

SITOGE KNOSUDY
1039 S.E. FRANKLIN STREET
PORTLAND, OR 97202

⑆000123191⑆123 814004 3⑈

W

CURRENCY	
COIN	
*CHECKS BY BANK NO.	
1	
2	
3	
SUBTOTAL IF CASH RETURNED FROM DEPOSIT	
LESS CASH RETURNED FROM DEPOSIT	
TOTAL DEPOSIT ▶	

*FOR MORE THAN THREE CHECKS, LIST ALL CHECKS ON REVERSE AND ENTER CHECK TOTAL ONLY ON FRONT.

Western Bank
Mercer Head Office:
4127 W Jefferson Blvd
072-1000

NO.   428

24-12/0123

_____ 19____

PAY TO THE
ORDER OF_____ $ _____

_____ DOLLARS

SITOGE KNOSUDY
1039 S.E. FRANKLIN STREET
PORTLAND, OR 97202

_____

⑆000123191⑆123 814004 3⑈   428

W

BANK PRINTING COMPANY, INC

---

1. You want to open a checking account. What information do you have to give the bank? Fill out the first form.
2. You want to put $200 in cash and several checks you've received in your account. How would you do it?
3. You want to write a check to pay your hotel bill, which is $238.50. Make out the check to the Flamingo Motel. Sign your check with your full name and middle initial.

Activities

Explain the difference between the following words and expressions:

personal check/travelers check   gift certificate/warranty
cash/charge   sender/recipient
service charge/interest   telegram/night letter/telegraphic money order
to sign/to countersign/to initial   personal reference/employer
layaway/installment plan   to make out a check/to take a personal check

Test yourself 🖭

Listen to these words and phrases from Unit 6. You may already know them, but in the conversations they have special meanings. Match them with the words on the right that mean the same. Write the letters in the blanks.

1. .... Meet the deadline.
2. .... Will you okay it?
3. .... Write it up.
4. .... It's not the whole story.
5. .... My check bounced.
6. .... Ring it up.
7. .... As long as you have some ID.
8. .... I'm just looking.
9. .... I can get along without it.
10. .... It's a good way to carry cash.

a. Would you authorize it with your signature or initials?
b. The bank returned my bad check.
c. I don't need it.
d. I don't want any help.
e. Complete the receipt in writing.
f. It's a safe way to have coins and dollar bills in your purse or pocket.
g. There's more to it.
h. Get finished on time.
i. Only if you have some form of identification.
j. Record the sale on the cash register.

Which idioms would you use when shopping? When doing other business?

GETTING SOMETHING TO EAT

UNIT 7 ◁‖

PART I

A. Study these ads

B. Read

You'll find restaurants for every situation in the U.S. If you're in a hurry, you may just want to grab some "junk food" at a grocery store or a candy counter, or you can get a bite to eat at one of the many fast food chains, like McDonald's, Burger King, Kentucky Fried Chicken, or Taco Time. Or you can get a hero or submarine sandwich "to stay" or "to go" from a sandwich shop or deli. Some of these places have tables, but many don't. People eat in their cars or take their food home, to their offices or to parks. If you prefer sitting down but still don't want to spend much, you can try a cafeteria. At all of these places, you pay at a cash register before you sit down, and you don't have to tip anybody – but you usually have to clear the table when you finish!

Coffee shops are usually less expensive and less dressy than fine restaurants. So are pizza places, pancake houses, sandwich shops and family restaurants. But the name of a restaurant won't necessarily tell you much about the kind of place it is or the food it serves.

Like most fast food restaurants and cafeterias, many restaurants don't serve alcoholic beverages. This is often because they want people to feel comfortable bringing their children. Minors can eat at restaurants that serve beer and wine, but they are not allowed to enter pubs, taverns, cocktail lounges or bars. You may be asked to show some ID that proves your age before you go into a bar.

C. Answer the questions

1. What are the names of the restaurants in the ads?
2. What kind of food do they serve?
3. What hours are they open?
4. What meals do they serve?
5. Which ones serve alcohol? What makes you think so?
6. When does the pancake house serve lunch and dinner?
7. Where can you get food "to go"?
8. Which restaurant do you think is the most expensive? The dressiest? The most casual?

You can look up words on page 69.

D. Listen and answer

You will hear three conversations. In the first one, a man is calling a restaurant to reserve a table. The second and third ones take place at a restaurant. Listen first and then answer the questions.

1. Who answers the phone in the first conversation? What does Mr. Novak want?
2. What time does he reserve for?
3. What kind of restaurant do you think the speakers in the second conversation are walking into?
4. Why don't they sit down right away?
5. In the third conversation, why does the woman ask the man not to smoke?
6. Does he put out his cigarette?
7. When do you order a meal in a restaurant?

E. Listen and read

Two people who work together are on their lunch hour at a small restaurant near the office.

GEORGE: Hmm, there's not much on the menu here. The beef-kabob sounds good, though.

BECKY: Yes, it does, but I think I'm just going to have a sandwich today. Maybe even just half of one.

WAITRESS: Are you ready to order?

GEORGE: Yes, I think so.

WAITRESS: Do you want that on separate checks?

GEORGE: Oh, no, one'll be fine. It's on me today, Becky.

BECKY: Well – thanks, George. I'll treat you next time. Uh, I'll take half a French dip sandwich – go easy on the mayo – and I'll have a cup of coffee with cream.

GEORGE: And I'll have the beef-kabob.

WAITRESS: Okay. Anything to drink?

GEORGE: What kind of beer do you have?

WAITRESS: We have Schlitz on tap, and Löwenbräu, Budweiser, and Michelob in bottles.

GEORGE: A glass of Schlitz, please.

WAITRESS: Okay, and what kind of dressing would you like on your salad, ma'am? We have French, Thousand Island and blue cheese.

BEEF-KABOB

Best quality top sirloin cubes marinated in secret recipes and barbecued with special skewers on open fire and served with our own delicious hot sauce, rice and barbecued tomatoes. **3.95**

REUBEN

A combination of corned beef, white turkey, Swiss cheese, and sauerkraut with our own dressing. Grilled on rye bread.

½ . . . . . . **2.95**   Full **3.95**

FRENCH DIP

Thinly sliced cuts of roast beef layered on a French roll, with aujus, tossed green salad and chips.

½ . . . . . . **2.85**   Full **3.85**

CLUB SANDWICH

Thinly sliced turkey, bacon, fresh lettuce, sliced tomato and tangy cheddar piled high on three slices of toast. **3.95**

BECKY: Blue cheese'll be fine.

WAITRESS: Okay, thank you.

F. Answer and act

Listen to the conversation a couple of times. Make sure you understand the descriptions on the menu.

1. What does Becky want to drink?
2. Who is going to pay for the meal?
3. What comes with the beef-kabob?
4. What comes with the French dip?
5. What is in a club sandwich?

Read the conversation with two partners. One of you reads the waitress's part. The other two cover the page and order as Becky and George do. Trade roles. Then order whatever you want.

PART II

A. *Study this menu*

1246 W. Davenport
Dinners 5:30 – 10:30 Tuesday – Saturday
347-2981 for reservations

SOUPS

*Homemade, piping hot &
delicious*

Soup du Jour
Clam Chowder
Cup...$1.50   Bowl...$2.00

HORS D'OEUVRES

Tasty morsels before your meal

Shrimp cocktail	$3.50
Stuffed mushrooms	$3.00
Chicken livers in bacon	$3.50
Mushroom stuffed tomato	$3.00

SALADS

Shrimp Louie $4.25
*Tiny bay shrimp nestled
in our house salad*

Chef's Salad $3.95
*Tossed green salad with
slices of Cheddar and
Swiss cheese, thinly
sliced turkey and ham*

House Salad $1.50
*Sliced tomato and alfalfa
sprouts top this salad.
Choice of dressing*

WINES

*We are proud of our fine
selection of distinctive domestic
and imported wines. Please
consult our wine list.*

DINNERS

*Served with salad, vegetable du
jour, Idaho potato and a variety
of breads from our kitchen .*

Chicken Teriyaki $5.95
*Marinated in a mild sauce
and char-broiled*

Filet of Fish $5.95
*Halibut seasoned with
garlic and herbs and
served with our own dill
sauce*

Spareribs $6.50
*Sticky sweet and
delicious, marinated and
char-broiled to
perfection*

Prawns Orientale $8.95
*Prawns simmered gently
in a tasty ginger and
saffron sauce. Served
with rice*

Top Sirloin $10.50
*12oz. sirloin carved with
care, broiled to taste*

Top Sirloin and Shrimp $12.50
The best of both worlds

Prime Rib $12.50
*Our famous prime rib,
tender and juicy*

DESSERTS

Lemon cheesecake	$1.75
Buttermilk chocolate cake	$1.50

*Abernethy's features three or
four special desserts daily. Ask
your waiter about today's
delights.*

B. *Answer the questions*

1. What are Abernethy's hours?
2. Do they serve canned soups, or do they make them here?
3. Can you describe a shrimp louie in your own words? A chef's salad?
4. When do you eat hors d'oeuvres?
5. What comes with the dinners?
6. Which dinner comes with something instead of potatoes?
7. How many desserts do they serve here?
8. How can you find out about the desserts?
9. How can you find out about the wines they serve here?

C. Look and listen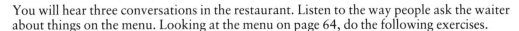

You will hear three conversations in the restaurant. Listen to the way people ask the waiter about things on the menu. Looking at the menu on page 64, do the following exercises.

1. You want to order the prime rib, but you don't like potatoes. Decide what you'd like instead and how you'd ask the waiter if you could substitute it.
2. You would like to order some beef. Which dinners can you choose from?
3. You do not like pork. Which things shouldn't you order?
4. You are out to dinner with an important guest, who you want to wine and dine properly. What would you say to the maître d' and what would you suggest your guest order?

D. Problem solving

1. You want to arrange a business breakfast for yourself and representatives of another company. Call the restaurant to reserve a table for the number of people and time you want. Ask what they have on their breakfast menu.
2. Ask someone about their favorite breakfast and dinner dishes. Find dishes on these menus that are similar or have some of the same ingredients. Write descriptions of your favorite dishes.

BREAKFAST

Abbot's Delight	3.60
hash browns, toast, avacado, scallions 3-egg omelette (tomato, sprouts, swiss, cheddar	
Decent Breakfast	2.60
2 eggs, hash browns, toast bacon, ham, or sausage	

3-egg Omelettes
w/ hash browns & toast

ham & cheese	3.10
ham	2.60
cheese	2.35
plain	2.00
Corn Beef Hash	2.30
w 1 egg & toast	

3-pancakes	1.40	hot cereal	.85	toast	.15
short stack	1.00	cold cereal	.45	muffin—apple-nut	.60
1-egg	.50	granola	1.49/.60	cinnamon roll—	.70
2-eggs	.80	yogurt	.85/.60	sweet breads:	.60
3-sausage	1.10	fruit salad	.95/.65	poppy seed	
3-bacon	1.10	frt. sal. & yogt.	1.30/.60	banana-nut	
ham	1.10			date-nut	
hash browns	.70				

HOURS

Mon-Fri 6:30 a.m to 9 p.m.	Saturday 7 a.m to 9 p.m.
(Breakfast until 10:30 a.m.)	(Breakfast until noon)

E. Asking about and describing food

Using the following pattern and working with partners, ask and tell about these things: coffee in your partner's country; their favorite dish; breakfast in your partner's country; their favorite restaurant or café; the grocery store or market where they usually buy food.

Ask about some kind of food or drink.

Accept it or turn it down.

Describe it.

PART III

A. Study these ads

These are ads for specials you would find in the newspaper. See if you can understand them.

B. Answer the questions

1. How much will the first can of MJB cost you?
2. How many different kinds of Sanka are there? Is the ground kind cheaper than

MJB decaffeinated? (Sanka is always decaffeinated.)
3. How much is a 3-ounce box of Jell-O?
4. What else is on sale?

C. Listen and read 📼

Here are two conversations that might take place when you want to go grocery shopping. In the first one, two people are looking in the paper to see what the specials are. They are making a shopping list.

JEFF: I've checked the kitchen and made a list of the things we're out of.

MELINDA: Okay . . . Kienow's has baked beans on special at 98¢ for a large can. Let's pick some up while we're there.

JEFF: Okay . . . We need some coffee – is there anything on sale?

MELINDA: Let's see . . . Yeah, S & W Colombian is on for $2.59 a pound.

That's pretty good.

JEFF: Sure is. What else have they got?

MELINDA: Popcorn's cheap – two pounds for 79, and I think we're out.

JEFF: Yeah, we are – I used the last of it on Sunday. Anything else?

MELINDA: Their TV dinners are on sale, too, but who cares?

JEFF: No thanks! Let's go!

The second conversation takes place at the check-out counter of a supermarket.

CLERK: Good morning!
JEFF: Hi! It's pretty quiet here for a Sunday!
CLERK: Well, it's still early.
MELINDA: Oh, darn, I forgot to get toothpaste! Where would I find it?
CLERK: Aisle 7A, top shelf, near the paper napkins.
MELINDA: Thanks . . . Here you go!
CLERK: Okay, that comes to $53.40 . . . out of $55 . . . there's 50, 75, 54 and one is 55. Thank you. Would you like someone to carry that out for you?
JEFF: No, thanks, we can manage.
CLERK: Have a nice day, now.

D. *Answer the questions*

1. In the first conversation, what three things does Jeff add to the list of groceries they need?
2. What do they decide not to buy?
3. In the second conversation, what time of day and what day of the week is it?
4. How much does Melinda give the cashier?
5. How much change does she get?

E. *Act out the scenes*

1. Read the first conversation several times with a partner. Trade roles.

2. Cover the text and say the exact words Melinda used when she
   – told Jeff the baked beans were on special.
   – told him about the coffee.
   – told him the popcorn was cheap.
   – told him the TV dinners were on sale.

3. Now act out the scene with a partner.

4. Read the second conversation several times with a partner.

5. Cover the conversation and tell exactly how
   – Melinda said she'd forgotten the toothpaste.
   – the cashier told them the price and counted out their change.
   – Jeff said they didn't need any help.
   – the cashier said goodbye.

6. Figure out which coins and bills the cashier gave them. Which bills might they have given the cashier? Work with your partner, paying and making change.

PART IV

A. Read

Here are some more helpful things to know.

In the U.S., people prefer waiting for a table to sitting with people they don't know. This means a hostess may not seat a small group until a small table is available, even if a large one is. If you are sitting at a table with people you don't know, it is impolite to light up a cigarette without first asking if it will disturb them.

At American restaurants, cafés and coffee shops you are usually served tap water before you order. You may find the bread and butter is free, and if you order coffee, you may get a free refill.

Soft drinks are sweet, carbonated drinks like Coke. Hard drinks are alcoholic, like whiskey, vodka, etc. They are served straight or on the rocks. In some restaurants you can bring your own wine. In some states, you can buy liquor at a restaurant to take home. Every state makes its own laws about the sale of alcohol. In some states, you have to buy it at a special state-owned store licensed to sell liquor. Most cities and towns have no rules about opening and closing times for stores or restaurants, though they usually do make rules for bars. Especially in large cities, stores may be open 24 hours a day.

Servings in restaurants are often large – too large for many people. If you can't finish your meal but would like to enjoy the food later, ask your waitress or waiter for a "doggie bag." It may have a picture of a dog on it, but everybody knows you're taking the food for yourself.

Supper and dinner are both words for the evening meal. Some people have "Sunday dinner." This is an especially big noon meal.

Tips are not usually added to the check. They are not included in the price of the meal, either. A tip of about 15% is expected, and you should leave it on the table when you leave. In less expensive restaurants, you pay your check at the cash register on your way out. In some, a check is brought on a plate and you put your money there. Then the waiter or waitress brings you your change. In some restaurants you can pay with a credit card, including the tip.

B. Compare

American English	British English
check/bill	bill
liquor	spirits
liquor store	off-licence/wine merchant
potato chips	crisps
French fries	chips
hamburger/ground beef	minced beef/mince
candy	sweets
roast	joint
broiled	grilled
grilled	toasted
can	tin
to do the dishes	to do the washing up/to wash up

GLOSSARY

add'l (adj): additional

appreciate (v): to be glad about; to understand the qualities of something

allergic to (adj): having an allergy to a certain thing

au jus (adj): served with the natural meat broth

bacon (n): a kind of salty, smoked pork with fat, often eaten at breakfast

barbecue (v): to grill meat over hot coals, often with spicy sauce

beef (n): meat from cows

bite (n): something to eat; a snack

bonus (n): a special sale item; something extra

bother (v): to disturb

broiled (adj): cooked under a fire or heat

brunch (n): a meal eaten in the late morning, a combination of breakfast and lunch

caffeine (n): a chemical substance, a stimulant, found in coffee, tea and Coca-Cola

candy (n): very sweet sugary food

carbonated (adj): CO_2 gas in soft drinks or mineral water

char-broiled (adj): grilled over hot coals, usually without sauce

check (n): a bill at a restaurant

combination (n): two or more things put together to make one

consult (v): to read; to ask for advice

cube (n): an object with six equal sides

cut (n): something that is the result of cutting, a piece of meat

darn (interj): a shout used to express frustration or anger, like "Oh, no!"

decaffeinated (adj): without caffeine

deli (n): short for "delicatessen," a shop where you can buy salads and cooked meats, and have sandwiches made

domestic (adj): made inside the country; not imported

dressing (n): a combination of salad oil and other ingredients to put on salad

dressy (adj): stylish; semiformal or formal

entrée (n): a main course in a restaurant

fare (n): food

grilled (adj): cooked with little or no oil

grocery (n): a store that sells food; food

ground (adj): made fine

ham (n): a kind of salty pork with little fat

herb (n): leaves from a green plant used to add flavor to food

hors d'oeuvres (n): the first course of a large meal; appetizers

hostess (n): at a good restaurant, the woman who greets and seats the customers

hot (adj): spicy

ingredients (n): everything you put in a dish when you are making it

Jell-O (n): a particular brand of gelatin dessert; the word is commonly used to mean any such dessert

junk food (n): snack foods that are not good for you

license (v): to give official permission to sell something

liquor (n): alcohol

maître d' (n): the headwaiter

manage (v): to do something without help; to get by

marinate (v): to let food sit, or steep, in a sauce for several hours to several days before cooking

mayo (n): short for "mayonnaise"

minor (n): a person younger than legal age, usually 21, sometimes 18

on sale (adj): the price is lower than usual; also "on special"

on tap (adj): taken from a large container or keg, not from a bottle, e.g., beer on tap

on the rocks (adj): served with ice cubes

pancake (n): a thin, unsweetened breakfast cake fried in a pan and usually topped with a syrup

party (n): a group of people, e.g., a party of four

plain (adj): without anything extra

pork (n): meat from pigs

prawn (n): a kind of shellfish, shrimp

premises (n): a house or building with the surrounding land; private property

prime rib (n): an expensive type of beef

produce (n): vegetables and fruit

rare (adj): cooked meat that is very red inside and brown on the outside

recipe (n): directions for cooking something

reg. (adj): regular

Sanka (n): a particular brand of decaffeinated coffee; the word is commonly used to mean any decaffeinated coffee

sauce (n): a tasty liquid put on other foods

simmer (v): to cook at a temperature close to boiling

sirloin (n): a kind of beef steak

skewer (n): a long, thin, pointed piece of metal for cooking meat

sliced (adj): cut very flat and thin

spareribs (n): rib-bones of pork with very little meat on them, barbecued or char-broiled with sauce

straight (adj): an alcoholic drink without ice or any other liquids mixed in

substitute (v): to choose one food item in place of another offered on a menu

taco (n): a Mexican sandwich with meat, lettuce, tomatoes and cheese in a piece of thin, flat bread

tap water (n): water that flows from a pipe or a faucet

tavern (n): a place where you can get beer and wine, and sometimes hard drinks

tender (adj): easy to chew

tossed salad (n): mixed green salad

treat (v): to pay for someone's meal or drink

turkey (n): a big bird that tastes something like chicken

upset (v): to disturb

variety (n): many kinds of things

REVIEW 7

This is part of a dining guide to restaurants in Boston and Cambridge, Massachusetts. Study it and Unit 7 carefully before you answer the questions below.

BOSTON

NAME, ADDRESS, TEL.NO.	TYPE OF FOOD	HOURS	PRICES	CREDIT CARDS	REMARKS
Athens-Olympia 51 Stuart Street (426-6236)	Greek-American fare Specialties: spinach pie, moussaka, lamb dish (wines & liquors)	L 11-3 D 3-11:30	$	A,M,V	Reservations accepted Friendly atmosphere Casual dress
Brandy Pete's 82 Broad St. (off State St.) (482-4165)	Cosmopolitan with interesting daily specials	11:30-9:00 Closed Weekends	$	NONE	All food "real" & fresh, made from scratch on premises. No reservations
Casa Romero 30 Gloucester St. (Back Bay) (261-2146)	Mexican food and drink (wines & liquors)	D 6-10 Sun-Th 5-11 Fri-Sat	$$$	A,M	Reservations accepted
Chart House (Waterfront) 60 Long Wharf (near Aquarium) (227-1576)	Seafood and steaks (wines & liquors)	D 5-12 Mon-Sat 3-12 Sun	$$$	A,D,M,V	Casual dress
English Room 29 Newbury Street (262-5566) (247-7231)	American healthy servings (NO liquor served)	L 12 on D 5-9:30	$	NONE	Family style, simple food done well. No reserva- tions.
The Parker House Parker's 60 School Street (227-8600)	American & Continental Cuisine. The home of the Parker House roll. Steak Diane recommended	L 11:30-2:30 D 5:30-11:30 SB Seatings: 11:30 & 1:30	$$$	A,C,D,M,V	Contemporary, elegant dining room. Piano evenings in lounge. Reservations accepted, Jacket and tie required, Wheelchair accessible. Free Parking for diners.

CAMBRIDGE

NAME, ADDRESS, TEL.NO.	TYPE OF FOOD	HOURS	PRICES	CREDIT CARDS	REMARKS
Iruna Restaurant 56 Boylston Street (868-5633)	Simple, traditional Spanish fare	L 12-2 D 6-9 M-Th 6-10 F-Sa Closed Sun	$$	NONE	Reservations accepted Wheelchair accessible
Joyce Chen Restaurant 390 Rindge Avenue (492-7373)	Different schools of Chinese cooking (wines & liquors)	L 12-2:30 D 12-10:30 Su-Th 12-11:30 F-Sa	$	A,M,V	Reservations accepted Free parking
La Groceria 853 Main St. (near MIT) (547-9258)	Italian cookery (wines & liquors)	L 11:30-3 D 5:30-11	$	M,C	No reservations
The Peacock 5 Craigie Circle (661-4073)	French Provincial Menu changes weekly	D 5:30-10 Tu-Th 5:30-11 F-Sa Closed Sun & Mon	$	NONE	Reservations recommended

Abbreviations:
L - Lunch	A - American Express	$ - Inexpensive (Most entrees under $6)
D - Dinner	C - Carte Blanche	$$ - Moderate (Most entrees $6 - $10)
SB - Sunday Brunch	D - Diners Club	$$$ - Expensive (Entrees often over $10)
BW - Bring your own wine	M - Master Card	
	V - Visa	

1. What would you expect to find on the menus of each of these restaurants?
2. Which ones could you take business partners to for lunch?
3. Which ones require formal dress?
4. Which ones could you take handicapped people to? Children?
5. Which ones are not too expensive for you? Can you pay with a credit card there?
6. Where would you feel most comfortable?
7. Decide on one of the restaurants. How and for when would you reserve a table? What do you expect it would cost for a full meal for several people? How would you pay?

Activities

Explain the difference between the following words:

breakfast/brunch/lunch/supper/dinner
raw/rare/medium-rare/medium/well-done
soft drinks/hard drinks
straight/on the rocks
to go/doggie bag

What kind of food would you expect to find at each of these?

sandwich shop
deli
fast food drive-in
cafeteria
coffee shop
cosmopolitan American restaurant

Test yourself 📼

Listen to these words and phrases from Unit 7. You may already know them, but in the conversations they have special meanings. Match them with the words on the right that mean the same. Write the letters in the blanks. (Some letters may be used more than once.)

1. .... I'll treat you.
2. .... I'll take your word for it.
3. .... It's on me.
4. .... What's it like?
5. .... Wine and dine your guests.
6. .... Who cares?
7. .... I'll let you know.
8. .... We're out of it.
9. .... Go easy on the mayo.
10. .... We can manage.

a. It isn't important.
b. I'll pay for yours.
c. We don't need any help.
d. Impress the people you've invited to eat.
e. I'll believe you.
f. Tell me about it, describe it.
g. I don't want too much mayonnaise.
h. I'll tell you later.
i. We don't have any left.

Which idioms would you use in a restaurant to invite someone to be your guest for a drink or meal? How would they ask about the various dishes?

PART I

A. Study these instructions

In this unit, you'll see the names of lots of diseases and conditions. Use a dictionary to help you.

ASPIRIN

DIRECTIONS for ADULTS (5 GRAIN TABLETS)
For relief of Painful Discomforts in the following conditions:

HEADACHES – Take 1 or 2 tablets with a glass of water every 4 hours, as necessary, up to 12 tablets a day.

COLDS – FLU – To relieve painful discomforts and reduce the fever, take 1 or 2 tablets with a glass of water (or fruit juice) every 4 hours, as necessary, up to 12 tablets a day.

MUSCULAR ACHES AND PAINS – Take 1 or 2 tablets with a glass of water every 4 hours, as necessary, up to 12 tablets a day.

TOOTHACHE – EXTRACTIONS – or for relief of other pains following dental work, take 1 or 2 tablets with a glass of water every 4 hours, as necessary, up to 12 tablets a day.

ARTHRITIS AND RHEUMATISM – For the temporary relief of minor pains, take 1 or 2 tablets with a glass of water every 4 hours, as necessary, up to 12 tablets a day. *Caution* – If pain persists for more than 10 days, or redness is present, or in conditions affecting children under 12 years of age, consult a physician immediately.

BURSITIS – LUMBAGO – SCIATICA – For the temporary relief of minor pains, take 1 or 2 tablets with a glass of water every 4 hours, as necessary, up to 12 tablets a day.

SORE THROAT DUE TO A COLD AND FOR RELIEF OF MINOR THROAT IRRITATIONS – To relieve pain and discomfort, take 1 or 2 tablets with a glass of water every 4 hours, as necessary, up to 12 tablets a day.

MENSTRUAL PAIN – For relief of functional menstrual pain, headache and pain due to cramps, take 1 or 2 tablets with a glass of water every 4 hours, as necessary, up to 12 tablets a day.

NEURALGIA – NEURITIC PAIN – Take 1 or 2 tablets with a glass of water every 4 hours, as necessary, up to 12 tablets a day.

SLEEPLESSNESS – When caused by minor painful distress or discomfort, take 1 or 2 tablets with a glass of water at bedtime.

IF YOUR PRODUCT HAS A CHILD GUARD CAP.
TO OPEN: Line up arrows on cap and bottle, push cap up with thumb.
TO CLOSE: Snap cap on securely – do not line up arrows.

DIRECTIONS for CHILDREN
(5 GRAIN TABLETS)
To be administered only under adult supervision
For relief of Headache, Muscular Aches and Pains and the painful discomforts and fever due to Colds and Flu.

Under 2 years. . .	consult your physician
2 to 3 years.	½ tablet
4 to 5 years.	¾ tablet
6 to 8 years	1 tablet
9 to 10 years	1¼ tablets
11 years	1½ tablets
12 & over	1-2 tablets

Take with a glass of water or fruit juice. Indicated dosage may be repeated every 4 hours, as many as 5 times a day. Larger dosage may be prescribed by your physician.

NOTE: Your physician may prescribe larger dosages, for various conditions, when needed.

WARNING: Keep this and all medicines out of children's reach. In case of accidental overdose, contact a physician immediately.
THE BAYER COMPANY, GLENBROOK LABORATORIES, DIVISION OF STERLING DRUG INC., NEW YORK, N.Y. 10016

Information correct 1983.

B. Read

Getting sick away from home is a very frightening thought, but it's something you can sometimes be prepared for. Unless you are planning to move to the United States, check with your country's own health services or your health insurance agency before you leave home. Ask them what kind of treatment and what drugs they will pay for, what kind of receipts, bills or information they will want from the American doctor or hospital that treats you, and find out the deadline for sending these things in.

People who take medication regularly should bring enough with them for their entire stay. Pharmacists in one town will not fill prescriptions from other towns, nor those from other countries. If you run out of medicine while you're in the U.S., you'll have to be examined by a doctor and get a new prescription, Rx, written.

Some medication – such as aspirin and other mild painkillers, cold medicines and nasal decongestants, vitamins, cough syrups and sore throat tablets, Alka Seltzer or Pepto Bismal for indigestion or nausea, or Kaopectate for diarrhea – is available without a prescription. You can get these drugs over the counter at drugstores and supermarkets.

But what if you suddenly get sick, or if you have an accident? You can look under Physicians in the Yellow Pages and call a few doctors in General or Family Practice until you find one whose office hours are convenient for you and who has time to see you. It may be easier to go to a hospital emergency room, though it is usually more expensive. If you're too sick to do this, you can call an ambulance. You can find the emergency number on every pay phone.

C. Answer the questions

1. Do these instructions apply to children?
2. How many aspirin tablets can you take a day, at the most?
3. How many should you take at once?
4. Can aspirin reduce a fever?
5. You have sore muscles from playing tennis. Will aspirin help?
6. A dentist has just pulled an infected tooth. Will aspirin help the pain?
7. You have diarrhea. Should you take aspirin?
8. Without looking at the instructions, think of three discomforts you can take aspirin for.
9. Have you ever used aspirin? What was wrong with you?

You can look up words on page 79.

D. Listen and answer 🔊

You will hear three conversations. In the first one, a woman is sick in bed at home. The second and third take place at the doctor's office. Listen first and then answer the questions.

1. What's wrong with each of the three sick people?
2. What is the sick woman going to do?
3. Who is the first sick man talking to?
4. What does the man who has hay fever want?
5. What do you do to arrange an appointment with a doctor?

E. Listen and read 🔊

This woman hasn't been feeling well for a couple of days. She's decided to call a doctor.

NURSE: Doctor Kowalski's office.

SHEILA: Hi. My name's Sheila Berger. I'd like an appointment with the doctor as soon as possible.

NURSE: Have you been in before?

SHEILA: No, I haven't.

NURSE: Okay, you're a new patient then.

SHEILA: Well, yes, but I don't live here. I'm passing through town.

NURSE: I see. And what's the matter?

SHEILA: I'm dizzy and I have pretty bad diarrhea.

NURSE: Hmmm. Can you come in this afternoon at 3:00?

SHEILA: Uh-huh, that'd be fine.

NURSE: And since you're not a resident of Evanston, I'll have to ask you to pay the $55 for the office call today.

SHEILA: That's fine. See you at three.

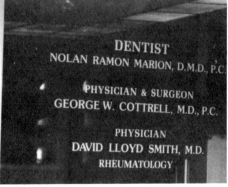

F. Answer and act

Listen to the conversation two or three times. Make a note of the appointment time and the doctor's fee. Then try to answer the questions without looking at the text.

1. When does Sheila want to see the doctor?
2. Is she a new patient? Why do you think so?
3. What is the matter with her?
4. When does the nurse want her to come in?
5. How much will the office call cost?
6. Is Sheila a resident of the town that Dr Kowalski's office is in?
7. What's the name of the town?
8. When will Sheila pay the bill? Why?

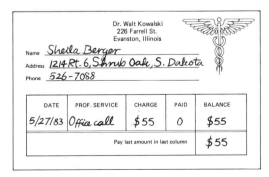

Read the conversation with a partner. One of you can read the nurse's part while the other covers the page and plays Sheila. Trade roles.

PART II

A. *Study this form*

MEDICAL HISTORY

HAVE YOU EVER HAD:
(Please circle yes or no)

German measles	Yes (No)
Venereal disease	Yes (No)
Date..	
High Blood pressure	Yes (No)
Varicose veins	Yes (No)
Blood clots in legs or chest	Yes (No)
Severe headaches (migraine)	(Yes) No
Heart trouble	Yes (No)
Kidney or bladder problems	(Yes) No
Diabetes (high sugar)	Yes (No)
Epilepsy (fits, seizures, etc.)	Yes (No)
Mononucleosis	Yes (No)
Hepatitis (liver infection)	Yes (No)
Date..	
Eye problems (other than glasses)	Yes (No)
Cancer	Yes (No)
Psychiatric treatment	Yes (No)
High Blood fats (cholestrol, etc.)	Yes (No)

Any other serious illness?.....................................
....
....

SURGICAL HISTORY

Have you ever had an operation?   (Yes) No
If yes, what type of operation and when?
...*Appendix*..
............................date.*11/24/76*.........
Any other comments?..
....
....
....

DO YOU TAKE ANY MEDICATIONS REGULARLY?
Yes ( ) No (X) If so, what?............................
ALLERGIES TO MEDICATIONS: Yes ( ) No (X)
If so, what?...
DO YOU SMOKE?   Yes (X) No ( )
If yes, how many per day?......*10-15*
DO YOU HAVE ANY MENTAL PROBLEMS IN YOUR FAMILY?
Yes (X) No ( ). If yes, what type of problems?
Who?.....*alcoholism — father*.........................

FAMILY HISTORY

Do any of the following diseases run
in your family?

Diabetes	Yes (No)
Varicose Veins	(Yes) No
Blood clots in legs or chest	Yes (No)
Cancer	Yes (No)
If so, where?..	
High blood pressure	Yes (No)
Heart Attacks (coronaries)	(Yes) No
Before age 50?	Yes (No)
Stroke	Yes (No)
Any other diseases?.....................................	

.........*Grandmother died of TB*.............
....
....
....

PREGNANCIES

Last menstrual period.....*6/3*......................
How many pregnancies?...*3*........................
How many births?......*2*..............................
Number of miscarriages?..*1*........................
Number of abortions?......................................
Any other comments?..
....
....

B. *Answer the questions*

1. Is this patient male or female?
2. Does this person take any medication regularly?
3. Is this patient allergic to any medications?
4. How many operations has she had? When did she have them?
5. Which health problems has she had?
6. What health problems run in her family?
7. Who died of tuberculosis?
8. Has this person had any children? How many?

C. *Look and listen*

You will hear three phone conversations with people who are not feeling well. Listen to the way they ask and tell about health problems. Looking at the form on page 74, write answers to the following questions.

1. Work out your medical history. Make a list of the diseases and conditions that you've had or have now. List the diseases and conditions that run in your family. Include the relationship to you of the person who has or had the disease.

2. All the illnesses mentioned in the medical history, except perhaps hepatitis, occur frequently in the U.S. Which ones are not common problems in your country? Which are?

3. Think of some serious illnesses that aren't listed here. Write them down and describe the symptoms. Are there cures for them?

D. *Problem solving*

You've had to go into Marquette University Hospital in Milwaukee, Wisconsin, for a minor operation. First, you'll be under observation for a couple of days. You haven't eaten anything yet. Together with your nurse, fill out this menu form.

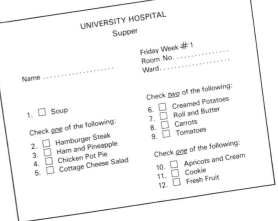

UNIVERSITY HOSPITAL
Supper

Friday Week # 1
Room No. . . . .
Ward . . . .

Name . . . .

1. ☐ Soup

Check *one* of the following:

2. ☐ Hamburger Steak
3. ☐ Ham and Pineapple
4. ☐ Chicken Pot Pie
5. ☐ Cottage Cheese Salad

Check *two* of the following:

6. ☐ Creamed Potatoes
7. ☐ Roll and Butter
8. ☐ Carrots
9. ☐ Tomatoes

Check *one* of the following:

10. ☐ Apricots and Cream
11. ☐ Cookie
12. ☐ Fresh Fruit

E. *Talking about health*

Using the following pattern and working with a partner, ask or tell about these problems: the flu, a bad sore throat, a broken leg, stomach pains, an allergy to antibiotics, food poisoning, an operation you are recovering from, an operation you are going to have.

Say hello and ask about health

Reply and explain problem

Offer help.

Accept or turn down help.

PART III

A. Study this information

This is part of a health coverage plan an employer might offer his employees in an American company. See if you can understand it.

When you Become Eligible

You are eligible for the program if you are a full-time employee. All salaried, professional and administrative employees are eligible on the date of employment. All other employees are eligible after the completion of 90 days' continuous service.

How You Become Covered

You will be given an enrollment card to complete. This enrollment card serves to enroll you in the Plan. This card must be completed within 31 days after you are eligible or evidence of good health will be required.

Coverage for Your Dependents

When you are covered under the Plan, you can also cover your eligible dependents. If both you and your spouse participate in the Plan, either but not both of you may cover the children.

How to Cover Dependents

The enrollment of your dependents is voluntary. A monthly fee will be charged to you through payroll deduction should you elect dependent protection. Dependents' coverage cannot begin under the Plan until your own coverage becomes effective.

How to Claim Benefits

Benefits payable under the basic hospital coverage will be paid to the hospital.
Have your physician submit the standard physician's claim form. You must then complete a claim form which can be obtained from the personnel department. You do not need to wait until the end of a calendar year to claim benefits. As charges begin to accumulate, you may file your Major Medical claims during the period services are being provided. In any case, you <u>should</u> file your claim within 90 days of the end of the calendar year.

Be sure to always keep a written record of all medical services provided. Include the type of service, the date it was received, and who provided it. You will need this information for claiming Major Medical benefits.

B. Answer the questions

1. When does health insurance coverage begin for new employees?
2. How do you enroll in the plan?
3. Do you have to pay for your children's insurance?
4. When do you file your claims?

C. Listen and read 📼

Here are two conversations that could take place in a hospital emergency room.

DOCTOR: Hi! I'm Dr. Crawford. What's the problem?
CAROL: I fell down some steps and hurt my wrist.
DOCTOR: I'll say you did. That looks pretty swollen. Let's see . . . Does that hurt?
CAROL: Ow!
DOCTOR: Can you move it at all?
CAROL: It hurts too much!
DOCTOR: Does it hurt when I bend it?
CAROL: Yes!
DOCTOR: It may be broken, or it may be badly sprained. I'm going to have an X-ray taken, and then we'll see. I'll probably want to put a cast on it. In the meantime, I'll give you something for the pain. Are you allergic to any drugs?
CAROL: No.
DOCTOR: Okay, take these, and then go to X-ray, two doors down the hall. The nurse will help you.
CAROL: Thanks.

The second patient is feeling nauseous.

DOCTOR: Hi! What's the trouble?

RICK: I've got diarrhea and I've been throwing up.

DOCTOR: When did it start?

RICK: Night before last.

DOCTOR: Have you been taking anything for it?

RICK: Yes, Kaopectate, but it's not getting any better.

DOCTOR: Did the nurse take your temperature? Oh, yes, I see . . . it was normal. Do you have any pains? Any muscular soreness?

RICK: No, I can't say that I do.

DOCTOR: Anything else?

RICK: Yeah, I feel light-headed, sometimes even a little dizzy.

DOCTOR: Well, it's probably some kind of influenza, but it could be mild food poisoning. Have you eaten anything that tasted unusual lately?

RICK: Well, no, not really. I'm not used to the food in this part of the country, but it all tasted pretty good to me. I don't think anything I ate was spoiled.

DOCTOR: Well, I'm sure it's nothing to worry about, but I'd like to run some tests to make sure it's not something more serious.

RICK: That's fine with me.

D. Answer the questions

1. Why does Carol have to have X-rays taken?
2. Does the doctor give her anything to stop the pain?
3. What's wrong with Rick?
4. Could it have been something he ate?

E. Act out the scenes 👥

1. Read the first conversation several times with a partner. Trade roles.

2. Tell your partner exactly how
   – the doctor asked what was wrong.
   – Carol told him what was wrong.
   – the doctor examined Carol's wrist and how she reacted.

3. Work with a partner. One of you read the doctor's part. The other play Carol – without looking at the conversation.

4. Read the second conversation several times with a partner. Trade roles.

5. Tell your partner exactly how
   – the doctor asked what was wrong.
   – Rick told him what was wrong.
   – the doctor asked if Rick had been taking anything for his problem.
   – Rick described his symptoms.

6. Work with a partner. One of you read the doctor's part. The other play Rick – without looking at the conversation.

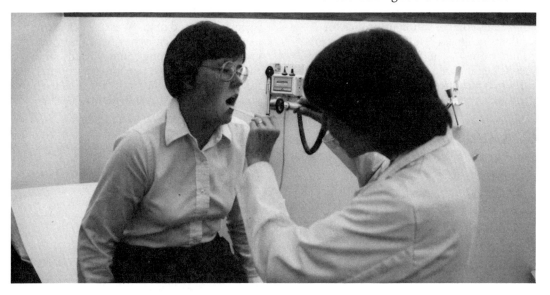

PART IV

A. Read

Here are some helpful things to know.

You should be prepared to pay for office calls, emergency room treatment and even hospital stays when you travel in the U.S., as most doctors and hospitals will want you to pay when you are treated. Hospitals usually require deposits of several hundred dollars or the name of someone who will promise to pay in case you don't. This is not just because you are foreigners – it's true for anyone who is not a resident of the area. Make arrangements with your health or travel insurance company before you leave, or take some extra money with you in case of an emergency.

Employees are covered through workmen's compensation insurance for accidents or illness resulting from their job from day one – even if health plan coverage doesn't begin until later.

There is a chance you can get medical attention at no cost. Whether free medical care is available – and who qualifies for it – depends on the city or county where you are. Call the local health department to find out about it.

Americans still use the Fahrenheit system for measuring temperature. Normal body temperature is 98.6 degrees; that's 37 degrees Celsius. A fever of 104 or 105 degrees is a very high one. Your temperature is usually taken orally.

North America has three plants that can cause skin rashes in people who are allergic to them – and many people are. They are called poison ivy (generally found in the East), poison oak, and poison sumac (generally found in the West). They are not usually found in cities or towns, but can grow on farms, along country roads, or in the mountains. If you go into the country, ask some people who know the area to show you how to identify these plants.

B. Compare

American English	British English
to get sick	to be taken ill
emergency ward	casualty department
doctor's office	doctor's surgery
operating room	operating theatre
shot/injection	injection/jab
druggist	chemist
drugstore/pharmacy	chemist's/pharmacy

GLOSSARY

ache (n): a continuous pain; (v): to hurt

allergy (n): the body's negative reaction to things, e.g., flowers or milk

ambulance (n): a large vehicle for carrying sick or injured people to the hospital

antibiotic (n): a medical substance made from living things and able to kill bacteria in the body

bacteria (n): very small living things, some of which cause disease; also called "germs"

bend (v): to force something into an angle

bruised (adj): having a sore (but not cut) spot on the skin; a *bruise* (n) may turn black and blue

call (n): a visit

claim (n/v): demand for money

clot (n): hardened blood that forms in the bloodstream and can cause danger to life

considering (adv): in view of; taking everything into account

county (n): a division of government smaller than a state and larger than a city

culture (n): a selected group of bacteria grown and studied in a laboratory

cure (v): to bring health to a sick person

diarrhea (n): loose bowels

discomfort (n): a mild pain or nausea

disease (n): an illness, discomfort or disorder caused by infection or unnatural growth

dizzy (adj): having an unpleasant feeling that things are going around and around, that your head is swimming, spinning

drug (n): a medicine; also a habit-forming substance

drugstore (n): a pharmacy or store that sells medicine, as well as beauty products, film, etc.

eligible (adj): allowed or qualified to do something

enroll (v): to register; *enrollment* (n): registration

extract (v): to pull out or remove; *extraction* (n): removal of a tooth

face (v): to look in the face; *face the facts* means to accept an unpleasant truth

fee (n): money you pay for professional services to a doctor, lawyer, etc.

file (v): to send in or record officially

flu (n): short for "influenza," a common disease with symptoms that include aching muscles, fever, diarrhea and nausea

hay fever (n): an allergy against the pollens of plants, with symptoms similar to a cold's

hot (adj): a slang expression for "good" or "well," used mainly in the expression "not feeling so hot," meaning that the person feels sick or depressed

indigestion (n): a condition in which the stomach is having trouble using or digesting food

infected (adj): red, sore and swollen because of germs in the body

itchy (adj): irritating the skin so that you want to scratch it

joint (n): a moveable part between two bones

Kleenex (n): a particular brand of paper tissue, commonly used to mean any paper tissue used for blowing your nose

lab (n): short for "laboratory", the place where scientists and technicians work

menstrual (adj): having to do with menstruation, a woman's monthly period

nasal decongestant (n): medication that opens up the nose, used when hay fever or a cold makes it difficult to breathe

nausea (n): the feeling you are going to vomit; *nauseous* (adj): suffering from nausea

operate (v): to cut the body open in order to treat some part of it

pharmacist (n): a person licensed to mix drugs and to fill prescriptions; a druggist

physician (n): a doctor

poison (n): a dangerous substance; also, "poisoning"

pregnancy (n): the condition of having an unborn child in the body

prescription (n): a written order from a doctor to a pharmacist to give drugs to someone

pressure (n): the strength with which something presses; e.g., blood pressure

rash (n): a condition in which the skin is sore and itchy, or has red spots

relief (n): what you feel when pain is gone

relieve (v): to make pain less strong

Rx (n): a symbol for "prescription"

sneeze (v): to clear your nose by a sudden uncontrolled burst of air

sore (adj): painful; *soreness* (n): pain

spoil (v): to lose freshness; to cause decay; *spoiled* (adj)

sprain (v): to turn a joint so that the muscles around it are sore and swollen; *sprain* (n)

stiff (adj): painful when moved

surgeon (n): a doctor who specializes in operating; *surgery* (n): an operation

swell (swelled, swollen – v): to become enlarged or fuller and rounder than normal

symptom (n): a change in the body's normal condition, the sign of an illness

tablet (n): a pill

thermometer (n): the instrument used for measuring body temperature

treatment (n): a method or substance used in treating a patient medically

venereal disease (n): an illness passed on by sexual activity; also called "VD"

virus (n): a living thing smaller than bacteria that causes infectious disease; also, the disease itself

vitamin (n): a chemical substance found in foods in very small amounts, but important for your health

vomit (v): to throw up food from out of your stomach

X-ray (n): a picture of bones under the skin and muscle; *X-ray* (v): to take X-rays

REVIEW 8

This is part of a guide to hospitals in Baltimore, Maryland. Study it and Unit 8 carefully before you answer the questions below.

**The United States Public
Health Service Hospital**

P.H. Mattingly, M.D.
Director

3100 Wyman Park Drive
Baltimore, Maryland 21211
(301) 338-3000
AHA & JCAH

158 Beds
Public Health Service Operated

NO PEDIATRIC OR OB INPATIENT SERVICES

Core services available. Highlights include:

- Alcoholism Service: a 24-bed unit provides medical and alcoholism coun-seling services in a 7-day program for both male and female community residents.
- Center for Occupational and Environmental Health in conjunction with The Johns Hopkins University provides screening, diagnosis and treatment of work and environment related illness.
- Geriatric Programs
  A. Geriatric Day Treatment Center; rehabilitation, medical and social servi-ces for referred senior citizens. Individual treatment programs by staff professionals.
  B. Community Geriatric Service provides medical/social assessment for elderly persons in the community, with linkages to primary care and social services as needed.
- Cardiology Department conducts cardiovascular research, operates diag-nostic laboratory and provides a comprehensive cardiac rehabilitation pro-gram, and coronary care unit.
- Psychiatry Department offers short-term inpatient and outpatient care, and in conjunction with North Baltimore Center maintains an emergency eval-uation and admissions program.

John F. Kennedy Institute for Handicapped Children

707 North Broadway
Baltimore, Maryland 21205
(301) 955-4500
JCAH
NO EMERGENCY SERVICES
Specialty, Pediatric Hospital.

Marvin Fitts
Administrator

40 Beds
Non-Government/Non-Profit

The Kennedy Institute is an interdisciplinary facility fully committed to advances in patient care, training and research. It is a short-term diagnostic, evaluation and habil-itation center which seeks to treat individually each child's specific or multiple handicaps.

Disciplines operating at the Institute include:

- Behavioral Psychology
- Child Development
- Genetics
- Hearing and Speech

Outpatient clinics include:

- Birth Defects
- Cerebral Palsy and Orthopaedics
- Diagnosis and Evaluation
- Pediatric Seizure
- Adolescent Seizure
- Lead Poisoning
- Movement Disorder
- Pediatric Neurology
- Neurodevelopmental Clinic

The Kennedy Institute also has a school for children with learning disabilities and a variety of community outreach programs stressing health education.

Provident Hospital, Inc.

Thomas W. Chapman
President

2600 Liberty Heights Avenue
Baltimore, Maryland 21215
(301) 225-2000
AHA & JCAH

271 Beds
Non-Government/Non-Profit

A 271-bed facility founded June 13, 1894.
Core services available. Highlights include:

- First hospital in Maryland with Acute Stroke Treatment Unit using multi-disciplinary approach from day of admission.
- Sickle Cell Anemia Project—a service-oriented program providing the greater Baltimore area with education, screening and counseling on sickle cell anemia and other hemoglobinopathies. Additional services include fol-lowup care, accommodating sickle cell patients through the use of a prim-ary care clinic, handling of referrals from area hospitals and cross referrals with other city based sickle cell programs.
- OB/GYN Department with fetal monitoring and laparoscopy.
- Tel-Med—A free telephone health information service providing over 300 medically approved tape-recorded health messages. The tapes are designed to provide up-to-date medical information to callers to identify early signs of illness. The system is not designed to replace the services of a physician, to diagnose an illness or to be used in an emergency.
- Infectious Diseases—Specializes in expertise in the identification and man-agement of infections. Consultant to community physicians in planning antibiotic therapy and in identifying microbial infections.

Good Samaritan Hospital

James A. Oakey
President

5601 Loch Raven Boulevard
Baltimore, Maryland 21239
(301) 323-2200
AHA, JCAH, CARF & CHA
NO EMERGENCY SERVICES

253 Beds
Non-Government/Non-Profit

Core services, except pediatrics and obstetrics, available.

- Medical, surgical and specialty outpatient clinics available.
- Specialty services in rheumatology, rehabilitation medicine, orthopaedics, clinical immunology and renal medicine.

The Johns Hopkins Hospital

Robert M. Heyssel, M.D
Executive Vice President
& Director

600 North Wolfe Street
Baltiore, Maryland 21205
(301) 955-5000
AHA & JCAH

1136 Beds
Non-Government/Non-Profit

EMERGENCY SERVICES include separate pediatric emergency facility
Core services available. Highlights include:

- Open heart surgery.
- Corneal transplant.
- Kidney dialysis and transplant.
- The Wilmer Eye Institute.
- The Phipps Psychiatric Institute.
- 200-bed Children's Center.
- The Woman's Clinic.
- Pediatric Trauma Referral Center (part of the Emergency Medical Services sys-tem) specially designed to handle both newborn and pediatric trauma emergencies.
- Regional Center.
- Hearing and Speech Center.
- Outpatient service in primary and specialty clinic.

---

1. In which of these hospitals could a woman have a baby delivered?
2. Which of these hospitals do not treat children?
3. Which hospital is the largest?
4. Which hospital would you not go to in an emergency?
5. Which hospital specializes in occupational and environmental health problems?
6. What's the best hospital to go to if you think you have an unusual virus?

Activities

Describe the symptoms of these diseases and disorders:

a cold
food poisoning
hay fever
appendicitis
flu
a sprain

Explain the difference between the following:

X-rays/throat culture
swollen/broken/sprained
wrist/ankle
disease/disorder

Test yourself

Listen to these words and phrases from Unit 8. You may already know them, but in the conversations they have special meanings. Match them with the words on the right that mean the same. Write the letters in the blanks.

1. .... Sit tight!

2. .... It hurts like hell!

3. .... I can't keep anything down.

4. .... What's the matter?

5. .... It's your turn.

6. .... I'm coming down with something.

7. .... You might as well forget it.

8. .... It upsets my stomach.

9. .... Take something for it.

10. .... I'm not feeling too hot.

a. I'm getting sick.
b. I'm feeling bad.
c. Treat it with medicine.
d. Keep your seat and wait.
e. Don't even think about it.
f. It's very painful.
g. You're next.
h. I keep throwing up after eating or drinking.
i. What's wrong?
j. It makes me feel nauseous.

Which idioms would you use when talking about getting sick? About being sick?

ENJOYING YOUR FREE TIME

UNIT 9

PART 1

A. Study these listings

New York Times

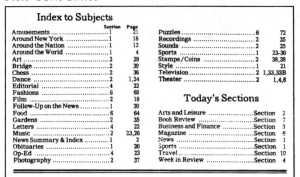

```
Index to Subjects
                        Section  Page
Amusements ...................1      21
Around New York .............1      18
Around the Nation ...........1      12
Around the World ............1       4
Art .........................2      29
Bridge ......................2      39
Chess .......................2      36
Dance .......................2    1,24
Editorial ...................4      22
Fashions ....................6      68
Film ........................2      19
Follow-Up on the News .......1      20
Food ........................6      64
Gardens .....................2      35
Letters .....................4      22
Music .......................2   23,26
News Summary & Index ........1       2
Obituaries ..................1      20
Op-Ed .......................4      23
Photography .................2      37

Puzzles .....................6      72
Recordings ..................2      25
Sounds ......................2      25
Sports ......................1   23-30
Stamps/Coins ................2   38,38
Style .......................1      21
Television ..................2 1,33,33B
Theater .....................2   1,4,6

        Today's Sections
Arts and Leisure ..........Section  2
Book Review ...............Section  7
Business and Finance ......Section  3
Magazine ..................Section  6
News ......................Section  1
Sports ....................Section  1
Travel ....................Section 10
Week in Review ............Section  4
```

Village Voice

```
A D V E R T I S I N G   L I S T I N G S

Art/Galleries............. 101
Books .................... 53
Cafes/Clubs/Discos ....... 114
Classified ............... 123
Concerts ................. 86
Curious Gift Guide ....... 71
Dining Out............... 112
Film..................... 60
Mind/Body/Spirit ........ 57
Loft Directory .......... 134
Personal Care ........... 38
Schools ................. 50
Skiing................... 44
Vacation/Travel ......... 55

Dance Events............ 98
Galleries................ 122
On & Off Broadway/Off-
  Off Broadway.......... 110
Village Movies/Manhattan
  Movies/Other Movies... 64
```

B. Read

Here are indexes from two New York City papers – the *Village Voice*, a weekly, and the *New York Times*, a daily. Usually you can find the index, or table of contents, on the front page of a newspaper.

A daily newspaper is a good place to look for radio and TV schedules, and ads for movies and concerts. Some papers have lists of other events, too – football, soccer and baseball games, or bike rides and nature hikes organized by the local parks department, for example. But some daily papers list only a few of these events, so you should also pick up a copy of the weekly paper that most cities have, or the university paper if you're in a college town. These papers usually have more complete listings of what's happening around town.

Shoppers should know that store hours vary widely, even within one city. Generally, large stores open at 9:30 or 10:00 and close at 5:30 or 6:00 Monday through Saturday. Many shops open later. In most cities, there is one night a week when stores stay open until 9:00, usually Thursday or Friday. And many are open on Sunday afternoon for a few hours. Check ads in the paper to find out what the hours are.

In addition to newspapers, hotels are good places to get information. Some have calendars of events they give free to their guests, and the clerks will usually help you find out what you want to know. They can also tell you what sights there are to see. If you're driving across the country or through a city, you can also check the billboards you'll see along the roads. They advertise not only products but also coming events and sights to see.

C. Answer the questions

1. Where can you find a list of all the movies playing in New York? What about the plays on Broadway? What about those Off Broadway?
2. Where should you look in the *Voice* if you want to see a ballet?
3. Does the *Voice* have a TV schedule? Does the *Times*?
4. You're in New York and you want to go dancing. Where can you find some places to go?
5. Do both papers have information about art? Which pages is it on?
6. What are you most interested in? Where would you find information about it?

You can look up words on page 89.

D. Listen and answer

You will hear a conversation that takes place in a married couple's home. The woman's parents are visiting. Listen first and then answer the questions.

1. What city are these people in?
2. What is their problem?
3. How are they going to solve it?
4. Where can you find the schedule of TV programs?

E. Listen and read

Two people are in their hotel room after a busy day of sightseeing and shopping. Marge is reading *TV Guide*, a weekly magazine that includes schedules of network TV programs.

ART: What's on TV tonight?

MARGE: Well, there's *Love Boat*.

ART: Spare me. What a stupid show!

MARGE: How about basketball? UCLA vs. Oregon?

ART: Not bad. But aren't there any documentary shows on? Something about Africa or wild animals or something like that?

MARGE: Boy, you're sure hard to please tonight. Let's see . . . how about Walt Disney?

ART: Ah, come on, we're too old for that.

MARGE: Well . . . there's a movie on HBO – *Scanners*. Never heard of it.

ART: Me neither. I'll bet it's a real bomb. Let's check out the cable guide . . . yeah, here we go. Channel 33 has *Melvin and Howard*. That's supposed to be a good movie, you know.

MARGE: Yeah, it is. Let's try it.

Saturday Evening Programs
See listings for details.

	8:00	8:30	9:00	9:30	10:00	10:30
2	King's Crossing		Love Boat (CC)		Fantasy Island (CC)	
3 **10**	Gerty Stein Is Back...		Movie: Mr. Belvedere Rings the Bell			
6	Walt Disney		Golden Globe Awards			
8	One of the Boys	Harper Valley	Barbara Mandrell		Billy Crystal	
12	College Basketball: Oregon at UCLA				News	Newsmakers
17A	World at War (8:05)		Movie: Walk on the Wild Side (9:05)			
22	Movie: La Dolce Vita (7:00)				It Takes a Thief	
ESN	NHL Hockey: Jets at Penguins (6:30)		Sports-Center	College Basketball: Long Beach State at Cal (Irvine)		
HBO	Boxing (6:00)	Movie: Scanners				Year That Was: 1981

Reprinted with permission from TV Guide® Magazine. Copyright © 1983 by Triangle Publications, Inc., Radnor, Pennsylvania.

F. Answer and act

Listen to the conversation two or three times. Then try to answer these questions without looking at the text.

1. What does Art think of *Love Boat*?
2. What does he think of basketball?
3. What would Art like to watch?
4. Why doesn't Art want to watch Walt Disney?
5. Does Art think *Scanners* is a successful movie?
6. Do Art and Marge find something they want to watch in *TV Guide*?
7. Where do they find something?
8. Why do they decide to watch *Melvin and Howard*?

With a partner, read the conversation a couple of times. Then look at the TV schedule and act out the conversation. Trade roles.

PART II

A. Study these concert ads

B. Answer the questions

1. Where are these concerts?
2. How can you get tickets to Keith Jarrett?
3. Can you get tickets to the *Messiah* at the box office? How can you get them?
4. If you order *Messiah* tickets by mail, who do you make your check out to? What else do you have to send?
5. Who is the conductor of the *Messiah*?
6. When is the Capitol's box office open?
7. How can you find out the ticket prices for concerts at the Capitol?
8. Can you still get tickets for all the Capitol concerts? If not, which ones are not available?
9. Can you take any drinks into the Capitol? How do you know?

C. Look and listen 🔲

You will hear three conversations. One of them takes place at the home of a friend, one at a hotel, and the third at a box office. Listen to the way people ask about what there is to do – especially about concerts. Look at the ads on page 84 so that you see which box offices and concerts the speakers are talking about. Then answer the questions.

1. You've decided you can't afford to spend more than $11 to see the *Messiah*. Could you get tickets for that amount at Avery Fisher or Carnegie Hall?

2. You're going to be in New York from the fifteenth of November through the twenty-ninth, and you want to see a rock concert. Which ones could you still get tickets for?

3. You were planning to see Keith Jarrett and have already bought two tickets to the concert. Friends have come to visit, so you'd like to charge three more tickets to your credit card. How can you do that?

D. Problem solving 👥

Your favorite sports are rugby and horse racing, but your traveling companion wants to see some baseball while you're in Seattle. Using this schedule, try to talk your partner into coming with you.

By Wanda Terry

Mariners—The M's vs. Detroit Tigers, 5/25-26; four chances to shut out the Boston Red Sox, 5/27-30; Milwaukee Brewers game benefits United Cerebral Palsy of Washington on 6/1; pre-game activities at 6:45. (Kingdome, 628-3300.) All games at 7:35, except Sun 7:05.

U.W. Twilight Track—Co-ed track meet. (Husky Stadium, 543-2230.) 5/27 at 5.

Star Track I—Annual state coed track meet, Class AAA and AA. (Lincoln Bowl, Tacoma.) Session I at 11:30am; Session II at 7. 5/28-29.

Martial Arts—Expo-championship. (U.W. Hec Edmundson Pavilion, 543-2246.) 5/29; eliminations begin at 10am, finals at 7:30.

World Class Rugby—England's national team challenges the U.S. Cougars, our all-star team, in their first tour of play in the States. (Pop Keeney Stadium, Bothell, 624-8983.) 6/2, kickoff at 6:30.

Longacres—Tacoma Handicap, 3 year olds, 5/30; Memorial Day Handicap, 3 year olds and up, 5/31. (Renton, 251-8717.) Post time: Wed-Fri 3:45, Sat-Sun-Memorial Day 1:15.

Soccer—Seattle Sounders vs. Chicago. (Kingdome, 628-3450.) 6/5 at 2:30; Senior Citizens Day tickets, $1.50.

E. Talking about what there is to do 👥

Using the following pattern and working with a partner, ask or give advice about what there is to do in or near your town. Talk about such things as concerts, movies, sports events, art shows, museums, zoos, excursions, tours, restaurants, places to go dancing, skiing, swimming and shopping, and a place to buy running shoes. Point out the sights you should definitely see.

PART III

A. Study this ad

Here is an ad for a special event in Seattle. See if you can understand it.

B. Answer the questions

1. What event is this ad for? Who can go?
2. Who is putting on the event?
3. How can you get tickets?

4. Do you think it's better to send cash or a personal check with your ticket order? Why?

C. Listen and read 📼

Here are three conversations that might take place when two young men go bar-hopping. The first one takes place outside a club with a dance band.

JAY: Okay, let's go in and pick up some chicks. You're getting too hung up on Laurie.

MIKE: Yeah, maybe you're right. But I never know what I'm supposed to say.

JAY: Just get them to dance and then find out what they're into. After that, it's a breeze.

MIKE: I hear you, man, but . . .

JAY: Come on, man, I know you can do it. Just watch me once and you'll get the hang of it.

The next conversation takes place inside the club.

JAY: Hi, I'm Jay. Want to dance?
MEG: No, thanks.
JAY: Aw, come on.
MEG: I said no thanks. Now get lost!
JAY: Okay, okay . . . Hi, I'm Jay. What's your name?
KAREN: Karen.
JAY: Hi, Karen. You want to dance?
KAREN: Yeah, okay, why not?

 Mike has been dancing with Annette and now they're at the bar.

BARTENDER: Two drafts. That's two bucks.
MIKE: Here you go.
ANNETTE: Thanks, Mike. Hey, you know, you can really dance! That was a real trip! What sign are you, anyway?
MIKE: Uh, I think I'm a Taurus. How about you?
ANNETTE: Me? I'm an Aries. Can't you tell?
MIKE: Uh, well, no . . .
ANNETTE: Got a light?
MIKE: Oh, sure, here. You know, you dance real nice, too.
ANNETTE: You like it? You know, you really turn me on. Let's get out of here. I don't live too far from here and I've got some fantastic tunes at home.
MIKE: Well, I don't know. I'm here with a friend . . .
ANNETTE: That's all right. I get the message.

See you around and thanks for the beer.
JAY: Look, that was quite a chick. What happened?
MIKE: Aw, she wasn't my type. How are you doing?
JAY: Look, this joint's a real bummer. Let's move on.
MIKE: Anytime, man, anytime.

D. Answer the questions

1. Why do Jay and Mike want to go bar-hopping?
2. Are Jay and Meg polite to each other or not? What makes you think so?
3. What does the bartender bring Mike and Annette?
4. What does Annette want to do? What about Mike?
5. Why does Jay want to go somewhere else?

E. Act out the scenes 👥

1. Read the first conversation several times with a partner. Trade roles.

2. Cover the text and tell exactly how
   – Mike said he didn't know what to say to women.
   – Jay told Mike what to do.
   – Mike said he understood.

3. Now act out the scene with a partner. (If you and your partner are women, you can use the same expressions except you should use "guys" instead of "chicks.")

4. Read the third conversation a few times with a partner.

5. Cover the conversation and tell exactly how
   – Annette asked Mike to light her cigarette.
   – she told him she liked him.
   – she suggested that they go to her house.
   – Mike told her he didn't want to go.
   – Jay suggested that he and Mike leave.

PART IV

A. Read

Here are some more helpful things to know.

Theater, dance, opera and other organizations often put on events to raise money. These are "fund-raising" events. The organizations use the money to help pay their operating costs, which helps keep ticket prices down.

In certain states when you go to movies, theater, opera or concert performances, you may not be able to get alcoholic beverages in the intermissions. In most movie theaters, you can watch the movie as many times as you want at no extra charge. Smoking is allowed in specified sections of some movie theaters.

There are three commercial TV networks in the U.S. – NBC, CBS, and ABC – that broadcast nationwide through local stations. Commercials may interrupt the shows as often as every ten minutes. There's also a noncommercial public network – PBS. In addition to these, most towns and cities have cable TV, which costs a few dollars a month. At a hotel, you should be able to get five to twenty TV stations and at least fifteen radio stations, each playing a different kind of music. Most radio and TV stations broadcast at least eighteen hours a day.

Most TV stations have local news and weather before national and international news, which is at 6 p.m. except in the Central Time Zone. All national shows are one hour earlier there. "Prime time" is 8:00 to 11:00 p.m. This is the time when the most people watch TV, so the networks put their best shows on then. Radio stations usually have five minutes of news on the hour, though many cities have all-news stations which broadcast news 24 hours a day.

A big problem when you're out sightseeing or shopping is where to find a restroom. (That's a polite word for toilet.) Few cities in the U.S. have public ones, except in parks. Other places to find them are department stores, gas stations, restaurants and fast-food places with indoor seating.

Many people think that cities in the U.S. are dangerous. Though it's true that they are more dangerous than many foreign cities, it isn't likely that anything will happen to you. Ask a friend who knows the city or the clerk at your hotel if the neighborhoods near you are safe to walk in after dark. One of the most common crimes is purse-snatching, so if you're carrying one, hold it under your arm so it's difficult to grab.

B. Compare

American English	British English
vacation	holiday
movie theater	cinema
intermission	interval
guy	chap/bloke
billboard	hoarding

GLOSSARY

advertisement (n): a notice or display in a public place about a product, store or event that should make you want to buy, visit or attend

affiliated (adj): closely associated or connected

afford (v): to have enough money to buy something

apparently (adv): as it appears; seemingly

Aries (n): the first sign of the Zodiac, represented by a male sheep, or ram

bar-hopping (n): going from bar to bar

be into something (v): be interested in something

be turned on (v): to be excited; to like someone in a spontaneous, excited way

billboard (n): a large outdoor board for ads

bomb (n): a slang expression for "failure" or "disaster"

box office (n): the office of a theater where you buy tickets to shows and concerts

box seats (n): groups of more expensive theater seats, physically separated from the other seats, in which only 4 to 8 people can sit

breeze (n): a slang word for "something easily done"

broadcast (v): to send out radio or television presentations

Broadway (n): a famous street in New York City; most stage theaters in N.Y.C. were originally on or near it, and thus it can mean the theater district in N.Y.C.

bummer (n): a slang word for "disappointing failure"

cable TV (n): a pay TV system in which a station's signal is received through a wire (a cable) instead of through the air

channel (n): a television station

check out (v): a slang expression for "to go and investigate or find out more about"

chick (n): an impolite slang word for girl or woman

classified (adj): ads that are grouped according to their subject, e.g., all car ads are together, etc.

commercial (n): an advertisement on TV or radio

companion (n): a person you spend time with

conductor (n): a person who leads an orchestra or choir

documentary (n): a film, or radio or TV program that reports on a real event or facts

draft/draught (n/adj): beer on tap

dress up (v): to put on your better clothes

entertainment (n): public amusement, ways to enjoy yourself, e.g., dancing, going to movies, sports events, etc.

excursion (n): a sightseeing trip

fancy (adj): ornamental, requiring fine clothes

feature (v): to present something special

football (n): an American sport, different than the international sport called "football"

fund (n): a supply of money

get lost (v): a slang expression for "go away"

get the hang of (v): to learn to do something

get the message (v): to understand

guild (n): an association of people with similar interests

HBO (n): Home Box Office, a cable TV network that shows primarily movies

hear (v): a slang word for "to understand"

house (n): here, theater

hung up on (adj): being overly interested in or dependent on

intermission (n): an interval between periods of action, as between the acts of a play

joint (n): a slang word for "a boring or low-class place"

light (n): a match or "lighter" for lighting cigarettes

loft (n): an artist's living and studio space in the top floor of a building, especially in N.Y.C.

move on (v): to leave; to go somewhere else

movie (n): a film

muscial (n): a play or movie with a lot of singing and dancing

network (n): a national television company that produces or sponsors programs that are broadcast by affiliated stations in different cities. There are three main commercial networks in the U.S.

night life (n): the entertainment activities that are available at night

outlet (n): a location selling items made or supplied by a particular company

pickup (n): someone you meet casually, often at a bar, and often with the hope of a sexual relationship; *pick up* (v)

pub (n): a trendy word borrowed from British English for "bar"

purse-snatching (n): a crime in which a thief, on foot or on a bicycle or motorbike, takes someone's purse and runs away with it

recommend (v): to suggest; to give advice

sight (n): a place that is worth seeing

sign (n): short for "sign of the Zodiac"; one of the twelve horoscope signs

sold out (adj): having no tickets left

spare me (interj): slang for "I couldn't bear that"

sponsor (n): the person or organization that is responsible for an event

supported by (adj): helped with money or other important aid

Taurus (n): the second sign of the Zodiac, represented by a bull

theater (n): a place where stage plays or movies are shown

Ticketron (n): a company that has computerized outlets for selling tickets to entertainment events

trip (n): a slang word for "a lot of fun" or sometimes "unexpected fun"

tunes (n): songs; music

REVIEW 9

This is part of a tourist office's city guide to an American city you've always wanted to see.

EXCURSIONS

By Land

A Short Walk With History
9 Front St.   837-5424

Streetcar Museum
1901 Falls Rd.   547-0264

City Hall Tours
100 N. Holliday St.   396-1151

Gold Line
323-5510
Daily Sightseeing tours of the City beginning April 1.

Tour Tapes
110 W. Baltimore St.	752-8632
1401 W. Mt. Royal Ave.	462-4000
9 Front St.	837-5424
201 W. Monument St.	685-3750

Mini Tours
9811 Fox Hill Rd., Perry Hall   256-4533

The Touring Machine
1206 Longford Rd., Lutherville   823-6383

The Top of the World
27th Floor Observation Level, World Trade Center
Inner Harbor, Admission Charge   837-4515
Mon.-Fri. 10-5, Sat. 10-10, Sun. noon-5
A multi-media exhibit of the city's past, present, and future.

Old Town Mall, 400 and 500 blocks of N. Gay
Street. A bustling commercial area for over 150 years, this section of Gay Street was recently beautifully refurbished.

By Sea

Patriot II
685-4288
A tour by boat of the Inner Harbor, beginning mid-April. Daily at 11a.m., 1 & 3p.m.

ARTS

Arena Players, 801 McCulloh Street. Occupying newly renovated quarters, this dynamic group is one of the East's pre-eminent Black theatre companies. Box office 728-6500.*

Lyric Theatre, Mount Royal and Cathedral Streets. Fine acoustics make this the perfect hall for the Opera.
Box office: 837-5691.*

Center Forum
Old St. Paul's Church, Charles &
Saratoga Sts.   685-5537
A free noontime program of entertainment for all people. Tuesdays, Wednesdays and Thursdays, noon-1.30p.m. Nave Concert on Tuesdays.

Cinema Classics
400 Cathedral St., Wheeler Auditorium   396-4616
7.30p.m. Free
Mar.   **4** Room at the Top
     11 Cleo from 5 to 7
     18 Eclipse
     25 Only Two Can Play

INTERESTING PLACES

Aquarium, Pier 3, Pratt Street. The National Aquarium contains over 5,000 specimens of 600 different types of mammals, fish, birds, reptiles and amphibians in re-creations of their natural habitats. Ride on moving belts through a tropical rain forest, Atlantic coral reef, a gigantic shark ring and reproduction of Great Egg Island. Through September 14, Monday & Tuesday, 10-6; Wednesday-Sunday, 10-10. After September 14, Saturday-Thursday, 10-6; Friday 10-9. Admission charge. Call 727-3000.*

Science Center & Planetarium, 601 Light Street. Scores of fascinating displays, films, and learning experiences, focussing on everything from Earth to outer space. The planetarium should not be missed. Winter: Tuesday-Thursday, 10-5; Friday & Saturday, 10-10; Sunday, noon-6; Summer: Sunday-Thursday, 10-6; Friday & Saturday, 10-10. Admission charge. Call 685-2370. For 24-hour information, call 685-5225.*

Museum of Art, Art Museum Drive, Charles and 32nd Streets. Browse through permanent and special exhibitions featuring works from the old masters to contemporary art. The famed Cone Collection includes 19th and early 20th century paintings by Monet, Cezanne, Matisse, and Picasso. Plus, visit the Alan and Janet Wurtzburger Sculpture Garden. Tuesday-Saturday, 11-5; Sunday, 1-5; alternate Thursdays, 7-10p.m. Call 396-7101. For recorded information, call 396-7100.

The Block, 400 Block of E. Baltimore Street. This area has long fascinated those looking for neon lights, dark lounges, and "exotic" dancers.

1. Find tours to suit you if you
   – hate long tours.
   – love the water.
   – want to learn about the city's history.
   – like to hear a lot of details about what you're seeing.
2. Find entertainment to suit you if you
   – are a fan of old movies.
   – have free time at noon.
   – prefer theater to opera.
3. Find places to suit you if you
   – are interested in the stars.
   – enjoy night life.
   – like animals.
   – are studying art history.
4. You're in town for the weekend. Decide what you'd like to do. Be sure to write down the phone numbers.

Activities

Here are some informal expressions. Find another way to say the same thing.

It's a breeze.	This joint's a real bummer.
I'm into that.	Let's move on.
I hear you.	See you around.
Got a light?	Get lost!
That was a trip.	

Explain the difference between the following words and expressions:

index/schedule	hit/bomb
commercial/intermission	guy/chick
TV network/TV station	draft/bottled

Test yourself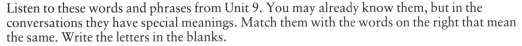

Listen to these words and phrases from Unit 9. You may already know them, but in the conversations they have special meanings. Match them with the words on the right that mean the same. Write the letters in the blanks.

1. .... Check that out.

2. .... I'm hung up on him.

3. .... You turn me on.

4. .... I'm hard to please.

5. .... You'll get the hang of it.

6. .... It's on the hour.

7. .... I'll talk him into it.

8. .... Let's pick up some chicks.

9. .... I get the message.

10. .... I'll bet.

a. I like him too much.
b. I understand what you mean.
c. I think.
d. I'll convince him.
e. Let's go meet some women.
f. I don't like very many things.
g. Find out some more information about that.
h. It's at the hour exactly (7:00, 8:00, etc.).
i. You will learn how to do it.
j. You excite me.

Which idioms might you hear when people are using slang to talk about the opposite sex?

BEING A WELCOME GUEST

PART I

A. Study this letter

> 52 Sutherland Road
> Omaha, Nebraska
>
> Dear Anne,
> Got your letter. Kenneth Moore told me
> about the hospitality you showed him when he
> was traveling abroad. This is just a quick
> note to say that yes, I'd be happy to see you
> when you're in the Omaha area. In fact, if you're
> in need of a place to stay, there's plenty of
> room here and I'd be happy to put you up
> for a couple of days.
> I'm in a hurry right now, so I'll be
> brief! I'll be in Omaha only through June 2nd
> or so. After that I'll be on a 3½ week business
> trip to Texas and the Southwest.
> Call me at work: 894-2055 or at home:
> 646-2915 (area code 402). It's easier to reach me
> at work. Just leave a message with the
> receptionist and I'll return your call in a
> couple of hours.
>
> Looking forward to meeting you!
> Sincerely,
> George Bates
>
> P.S. Please give my best regards to Ken if you
> talk to him again soon, and ask him to
> drop me a line!

B. Read

This is an invitation from a friend of a friend. While you're in the U.S. you may want to follow up on a name and address someone has given you. It's very possible that someone will invite you to a party, to their home for dinner, or even to stay with them.

People from different cultures sometimes do things that make each other uncomfortable – without meaning to or sometimes without even realizing it. Most Americans have never been out of the country and have very little experience with foreigners. But they are usually spontaneous, friendly and open, and enjoy meeting new people, having guests and bringing people together formally or informally. They tend to use first names in most situations and speak freely about themselves. So if your American hosts do something that makes you uncomfortable, try to let them know how you feel. Most people will appreciate your honesty and try not to make you uncomfortable again. And you'll all learn something about another culture!

Many travelers find it easier to meet people in the U.S. than in other countries. They may just come up and introduce themselves or even invite you over before they really know you. Sometimes Americans are said to be superficially friendly. Perhaps it seems so, but they are probably just having a good time. Just like anywhere else, it takes time to become real friends with people in the U.S.

If and when you stay with American friends, they will probably enjoy introducing you to their friends and family, and if they seem proud to know you, it's probably because they are. Relax and enjoy it!

C. Answer the questions

1. Who is inviting you to be his guest?
2. When's he going on his business trip?
3. How long will you be able to stay with him, if you need to?
4. What's the best way to reach him?
5. Did a mutual friend suggest that you write to George? Who was it?
6. Write an answer to the letter.

You can look up words on page 99.

D. Listen and answer

You will hear a phone conversation. A man is calling a couple he doesn't know. Listen first and then answer the questions.

1. Who are the speakers?
2. Where are they?
3. Why is Carl there?
4. Why is he calling Rose and Bill?

5. What are they going to do together?
6. What would you do if you wanted to stay at the home of a person you didn't know?

E. Listen and read

This woman has just arrived in Philadelphia to see the city and spend a few days with a woman she hasn't met yet. She is just knocking at the door.

JOAN: Hi! You must be Margo. Come in!

MARGO: Yes, hello!

JOAN: Did you have any trouble getting here?

MARGO: No problem. The directions in your letter were great.

JOAN: Come in, come in. I'm glad you looked me up. Put your things anywhere and sit down for a minute.

MARGO: Thanks.

JOAN: Do you have any special plans for tonight? There's a party, if you'd like to go. It ought to be a lot of fun – dancing and good food and stuff.

MARGO: Wonderful! I'd love to go with you.

JOAN: What do you feel like doing while you're here?

MARGO: Well, I'd like to look at the historic buildings.

JOAN: How about if I show you around the Old Town? You know, Benjamin Franklin and the Liberty Bell and all that, and we also have some pretty outstanding museums.

MARGO: I'm sorry but I'm not much of a museum person. But I do love old movies, so I'm open to that.

JOAN: We can check the paper. You know, the International House runs a really fine film program. I can get my schedule and see what's playing this week.

MARGO: Terrific!

JOAN: Hey, how's Bev doing anyway?

MARGO: Oh, she's fine. Nothing new – still doesn't like her job, but otherwise she's happy. Uh, another thing . . . do you think I could get some laundry done while I'm in town? I've been traveling for weeks . . .

JOAN: Sure, we can just throw your things in the machine. No problem.

MARGO: I'd really appreciate that. Say, do you think I could get something to drink?

JOAN: Oh, sure. The glasses are in the cupboard behind you. And there's some juice in the fridge, if you want. Just help yourself. Now, make yourself at home.

MARGO: Thanks.

F. Answer and act

Listen to the conversation two or three times. Then try to answer the questions without looking at the text.

1. Did Margo have any difficulty finding Joan's house?
2. What are they going to do tonight?
3. What does Margo want to see in Philadelphia?

4. What doesn't she like very much?
5. What things does Joan offer to do for her?
6. Does Joan get Margo something to drink?

Read the conversation a couple of times with a partner. Then cover it and try to act out a similar one using a city you know instead of Philadelphia. Trade roles.
Write a letter thanking your host or hostess for everything.

PART II

A. Study this appointment calendar

These are pages from a business woman's datebook with appointments for the whole week.

B. Answer the questions

1. What city will she be visiting?
2. How will she get there?
3. When will she arrive?
4. Why is she there?
5. How will she be getting around?
6. Where will she be staying?
7. What does she have planned for most of
   Wednesday, Thursday and Friday?
8. When will she be in Los Angeles?
9. What seems to be one of her main interests?
10. What are her plans for the evenings?
11. Is her trip being paid for? How do you know?

C. Look and listen 🔊

You will hear four conversations. Listen to the way people agree to suggestions – sometimes definitely and sometimes tentatively – and the way they sometimes try to get out of things politely. Look at the appointment calendar on page 94, so that you can see what days and times the speakers are talking about and where Tina will probably be at those times.

1. When will Tina be going to the art museums and galleries? Which ones is she interested in seeing?

2. Where should she write the golf date she made with Larry in her datebook?

3. Figure out when she will be having her heavy day and early night.

4. Which day or days will she probably be walking rather than driving around town? Why?

D. Problem solving 👥

Your itinerary looks just about as full as the one on page 94. In other words, you don't anticipate having much free time. But still you want to try to find time for your friends while you are in town. Call Sue and the Phildans to say when you'll be in town, that you want to see them, and then fit them into your schedule. If things don't work out, promise to see them on your next trip.

Tues. morning
Dropped by to see you but you're out. I really want to talk to you while you're in town. Please call me or come over for a chat.
Love,
Sue

Mr. and Mrs. Gordon Wallace Phildan
request the honor of your presence
at the marriage of their daughter
Leslie Anne
to
Mr. George Frederick Miller
on Saturday, the twelfth of May
at ten o'clock in the morning
Philbrook Art Center Garden
2727 South Rockford Avenue
Tulsa, Oklahoma

In case of rain
the ceremony will be held
at the Sheridan Avenue Christian Church
315 South Sheridan Avenue

E. Agreeing to suggestions or getting out of something 👥

Using the following pattern and working with a partner, suggest having a beer after work, going to a jazz concert, attending a formal reception, playing a game of golf, driving to El Paso, seeing a French film, going to a science museum and joining some business associates for a barbecue. Agree to some suggestions politely – sometimes definitely and sometimes tentatively. Try to get out of other suggestions politely.

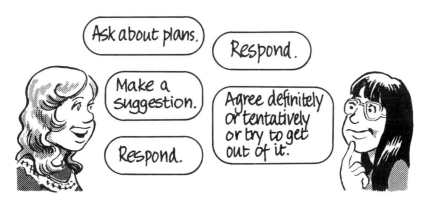

Ask about plans.

Respond.

Make a suggestion.

Agree definitely or tentatively or try to get out of it.

Respond.

PART III

A. *Study this invitation*

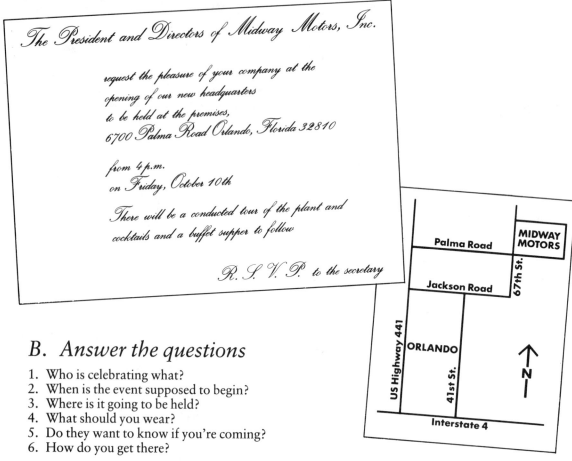

The President and Directors of Midway Motors, Inc.

request the pleasure of your company at the
opening of our new headquarters
to be held at the premises,
6700 Palma Road Orlando, Florida 32810

from 4 p.m.
on Friday, October 10th

There will be a conducted tour of the plant and
cocktails and a buffet supper to follow

R. S. V. P. to the secretary

B. *Answer the questions*

1. Who is celebrating what?
2. When is the event supposed to begin?
3. Where is it going to be held?
4. What should you wear?
5. Do they want to know if you're coming?
6. How do you get there?

C. *Listen and read*

Here are two conversations about parties. In the first one a woman is calling a friend to accept an invitation to a potluck dinner party.

JEAN: Hello?
ROBERTA: Hello, Jean? This is Roberta.
JEAN: Oh, hi!
ROBERTA: I got your invitation and it says R.S.V.P., so that's what I'm doing.
JEAN: Oh, good. Can you come?
ROBERTA: Yes, I think so, but Tony can't. He's got to go to his parents' and help them work on their house this weekend.
JEAN: Oh, that's too bad. It'd be fun to see you both.
ROBERTA: Yeah, well, some other time I guess . . . Uh, Jean, I won't have any transportation that night. I think I can get a lift over, but it's going to be a hassle getting home. Think somebody could give me a ride?

JEAN: Oh, sure! There's a bunch of people coming who live near you. I'm sure one of them would be glad to. If that doesn't work out, I'll drive you.
ROBERTA: Great! Thanks, Jean. Uh, what will people be wearing?
JEAN: Oh, most anything. It's a fairly casual party. We'll be in the yard, you know.
ROBERTA: Good! I can wear my new pants and sweater. Uh, it says "potluck." What can I bring?
JEAN: Well, a side dish would be good and a bottle of wine, maybe, but that's not really necessary cause there'll be plenty to drink and we're making punch.
ROBERTA: Okay, see you then!
JEAN: Bye!

The second conversation takes place at a cocktail party. Lois and Patrick work for the same company.

PATRICK: Lois, I'd like to introduce you to Alan Bernard, who's down here from company headquarters in Indianapolis. Alan, this is Lois McGrath from our marketing department here in Memphis.

ALAN: Pleased to meet you.

LOIS: How do you do, Alan. I hope you're enjoying your stay here.

ALAN: Yes, I am very much.

LOIS: What are you doing here?

ALAN: Well, I'm getting more familiar with our branches around the country. I noticed your office is very well run. I'd like to see more, but I have to be in Phoenix tomorrow.

LOIS: That's too bad! Where have you been staying?

ALAN: At the Morrison Hotel near here. It's small, but very nice. Great Southern hospitality! And the airport shuttle's just two blocks away.

LOIS: That's convenient! Taxis are so expensive these days.

ALAN: Yes. The company'd pick up the tab, but I don't mind the shuttle at all.

LOIS: Do you feel like something to drink?

ALAN: Thanks, but I'm afraid I'll have to take a rain check. But I'll be back in Memphis in five weeks. Maybe I could collect on the rain check then?

LOIS: Oh, I'd like that! Here, let me give you my card.

ALAN: That's great. Thanks!

LOIS: You're welcome!

D. Answer the questions

1. Will Jean's party be held outside or inside?
2. What kind of party is it?
3. In the second conversation, is Lois being too familiar when she addresses Alan by his first name?
4. Does she try to make Alan feel at home? How?
5. Does he take anything to drink? How do you know?
6. Do you think that Lois and Alan will meet again? Explain.

E. Act out the scenes

1. Read the conversations several times with partners. Trade roles.
2. Imagine you're at a party like one of these. Take the parts of the host or hostess and the guests. Your conversation should include these steps: a guest arrives; you introduce yourselves or each other; the host leaves the guests to themselves; the guests get into and out of conversations.
3. Try to meet someone you find attractive.
4. Thank and say goodbye to your partners.

UNIT 10

PART IV

A. Read

Here are some more helpful things to know.

When people in the U.S. have company or when they're invited to formal or informal get-togethers, they usually make a point of trying to make others feel comfortable and relaxed. On the whole, they tend to be informal. Men shake hands, but usually only when they're introduced. Male friends and business associates who haven't seen each other in a while may shake hands when they say hello. Women usually don't shake hands when being introduced to each other. When a woman and a man are introduced, shaking hands is up to the woman. Americans rarely shake hands to say goodbye, except on business occasions.

American women are used to being independent. They are used to going places by themselves, earning their own money, and often living alone. Sometimes they will ask men for help, but they usually don't want to be protected. Since the women's movement started, it's not always clear whether women expect men to open doors or help them into their coats. American women may start conversations with men or even ask them to dance.

There are a lot of Americans who don't smoke or drink, and many who don't want people to do those things in their houses. It's always best to ask before you bring alcohol to a dinner or before you light up a cigarette, if you're with people you don't know very well. Nonsmokers have become more militant about smoking in public places. Many restaurants, for instance, have established special sections for smokers.

House guests may bring gifts when they come to visit, and they often offer to help in some way. As a guest, you may want to ask your host or hostess if there's anything you can do to help in the kitchen. In many cases, the gesture is more important than actually helping. You may also want to take your friends out to dinner at the end of your stay, but it's not expected for you to do so.

B. Compare

American English	British English
vacation	holiday
rain check	postponement
yard	garden
Inc. (incorporated)/Co.	PLC (private limited company)
president (business)	managing director
ask for a ride	ask for a lift

98

GLOSSARY

address (v): to call someone by name

agenda (n): a list of items to talk about, especially at a meeting or conference

anticipate (v): to expect something to happen

appt. (n): short for "appointment"

attend (v): to go to

buffet (supper) (n): a meal in which all the food is set out on a long table. At less formal occasions, the guests usually serve themselves

bunch (n): a large number or a lot of

business associate (n): a person you know from business, usually an acquaintance rather than a friend

celebrate (v): to mark a special occasion by doing something special, e.g., having a party or going out to dinner

chat (n): an informal talk between friends

cocktails (n): mixed alcoholic drinks

collect on something (v): to receive what had been offered or promised for something

company (n): guests; also, a business firm

concl. (adj): short for "concluding"

confirm (something) (v): to make something firm or certain; to support

count on (v): to depend on

definitely (adv): without hesitation or doubt; with certainty

drop in (v): to visit someone without warning, informally

drop someone a line (v): to write someone a short letter

familiar (adj): informal, friendly

follow up (v): to take further action

formal (adj): according to accepted rules; dressed up

fridge (n): short for "refrigerator"

gesture (n): an offer to do something

get out of (v): to politely avoid doing something

hassle (n): a problem that requires effort to solve

headquarters (n): the main office of a large organization

honesty (n): truthfulness

hospitality (n): friendliness to guests

incorporated or *inc.* (adj): refers to an organization in which the people who actually own or control the organization are not held by law to be individually responsible for the actions of the organization

itinerary (n): a plan of a trip, including places to see and visit

lift (n): a ride

main strip (n): the most important street in a town; the street where most of the entertainment can be found

militant (adj): having a definite opinion about something and being willing to loudly and forcefully express that opinion

mind (v): to object; to be against something

mutual (adj): shared by two or more people; held in common

negotiations (n): talking to others to come to an agreement

open house (n): a party that is open to anyone who wants to come

over (adv): from one place to another; from here to there; to someone's house

pace (n): rate or speed

pick up (v): to meet someone and give him a ride

plant (n): factory

pls. (interj): short for "please"

point (n): special effort

potluck dinner (n): a meal in which each guest brings part of the dinner with the result that the assortment of foods can be quite varied; in some parts of the U.S. this is known as a "covered dish dinner"

preferred (adj): favorite; recommended

promote (v): to give someone who works for you a better job

punch (n): a hot or cold drink usually made with fruit juice and other ingredients sometimes containing alcohol

rain check (n): a ticket given when a promised item, such as a sale item in a store, is not available – the rain check can be exchanged at a later date for the item; the accepting of an invitation, but for a later date

receptionist (n): an employee who answers the telephone and greets office visitors

reps (n): short for "representatives"

R.S.V.P.: abbreviation for "répondez s'il vous plaît" or "please reply to this invitation"

run (v): to manage or operate or administer

rush hour (n): the time in the morning and late afternoon when people are going to or coming home from work, and the traffic on the streets is very heavy

schedule (n): itinerary; daily plan

session (n): a formal meeting of an organization

side dish (n): a dish that is not a main course, such as a salad or vegetable

spontaneous (adj): natural and unplanned

stuff (n): things

superficially (adv): not deeply, on the surface

tab (n): bill; *pick up the tab* (v): to pay the bill

take in (v): to observe; to see, hear and smell; to absorb

tend (v): to usually do

tentatively (adv): not decisively; hesitantly

terrific (interj): very good

thru (prep): short for "through"

visual arts (n): painting, sculpture, film, video

work out (v): to develop in a satisfactory way

yard (n): a grassy area behind or in front of a house

REVIEW 10

Test yourself 📼

Listen to these words and phrases from Unit 10. You may already know them, but in the conversations they have special meanings. Match them with the words on the right that mean the same. Write the letters in the blanks.

1. . . . . . . Do you feel like a beer?	a. I would like that.
2. . . . . . . I'll have to take a raincheck.	b. You can serve yourself.
	c. Relax and enjoy yourself.
3. . . . . . . Glad you looked me up.	d. I said I'd do it, but now I want to avoid doing it.
4. . . . . . . Just help yourself.	e. You decide.
5. . . . . . . Take it easy.	f. Would you like to drink some beer?
6. . . . . . . Don't count on me.	g. You shouldn't include me in your plans.
7. . . . . . . I'm open to that.	h. I'm happy you came to see me.
	i. Write to me.
8. . . . . . . I want to get out of it.	j. I would like to, but another time – not now.
9. . . . . . . It's up to you.	
10. . . . . . . Drop me a line.	

Which idioms would you use to make someone feel at home? Which ones would you use to express that you don't want to do something?

Check yourself

Look at the nine pictures opposite. Each one shows a situation where you could use "check," a word you've seen many times in this book. Some of its meanings are shown here. Put yourself in each situation. Then see if you can explain where you are and use the word "check" to say what you want to do.

Here is an example:

1. At an airport: "I was on flight 302. These are my bags over here. Here are my baggage claim checks. Could I have my luggage, please?"

1

2

3

4

5

6

8

7

9

TEACHER'S GUIDE

How to Survive in the U.S.A. aims to provide students with a practical knowledge of American English so that they can communicate and understand well enough to get along in the United States. They should be familiar with basic grammar and vocabulary*, as this is an intermediate level course.

How do you teach the course? To break the units down for 45-minute class sessions, you can teach one or two parts at a time, depending on the students' needs and attention span. For intensive courses, two 90-minute sessions per unit will probably be necessary. Although there are many ways you can present the material effectively, here is a suggested course of action:

PART I, consisting of sections *A* through *F*, sets the scene. Before students open their books, you could give a short English introduction to prepare them for the problem that the unit is concerned with.

A. *Study the illustration.* Students open their books and take a good look at the illustration (a piece of realia). Tell them where they would be likely to see something like this. Questions about new words, grammar, pronunciation, and the topic can be answered by other students or you, or the words can be looked up in the alphabetical glossary at the end of the unit. (The page number of each glossary is given at the bottom of the first page of every unit.) But first encourage students to try to guess or figure out the meanings of unfamilar words.

B. *Read the information.* Several students in turn read sections aloud. This text is about the illustration and the general theme of the unit. As before, questions about new words, etc., should be answered by other students, if possible.

C. *Answer the questions.* Several students in turn read and answer the comprehension questions aloud, or some of the questions can be assigned as homework. Students can work alone, with another student, or as a class.

D. *Listen and answer.* Students shut their books while you explain that they will be hearing a short conversation or two. They may not catch every word, but they should not worry – they should just listen for the overall message rather than for every detail. Before you start the cassette, you will probably want to lead into the recorded conversation 1) by first presenting key vocabulary so that they will know what to listen for; 2) by briefly setting the scene (the situation is described in the directions); 3) by asking students to listen carefully and figure out "who", "what", and "where" (the comprehension questions are the first questions listed under *D*). Then play the recorded conversations one at a time – several times if necessary. (Even if they cannot understand a conversation very well, it is not advisable to have them read it in the Tapescript, because this detracts from the listening task. It is better to play the recording several times until they can answer the comprehension questions.) If students have been concentrating on the general idea, they should be able to answer the questions. The last questions in this part are "transfer" questions. In some cases students will have to use their own experiences rather than what they heard in the conversations to answer these questions. A class discussion could develop. The "transfer" questions also lead into the next recorded conversation.

---

* as defined in the Threshold Level for Modern Language Learning (Jan van Ek and Louis Alexander, *Threshold Level English*, Pergamon Press 1980) and the General Service List of English Words (Michael West, Longman, 1953).

E. *Listen and read.* Students' books are still closed. Set the scene to get them to listen actively to the conversation. After hearing the conversation several times without following the text, students open their books and read along while you play the cassette again. As before, let students answer questions about new words if possible. Use the illustration to sharpen their understanding. Play the recording again, if necessary.

F. *Answer and act.* Several students in turn read and answer the comprehension questions aloud, or some can be assigned as homework. Students work alone, with another student, or as a class. In the last exercise, students read the conversation with a partner. Suggest that they exchange parts or "trade roles."

PART II, consisting of sections *A* through *E*, presents a problem to be solved.

A. *Study the illustration.* Students open their books and study the illustration carefully. Tell them where they would be likely to see something like it.

B. *Answer the questions.* Several students read and answer the comprehension questions aloud, or some can be assigned as homework. Students can work alone, with others, or as a class, using the new words to answer the questions.

C. *Look and listen.* Students' books are open to the illustration *(A)* on the opposite page. Explain that they will be hearing several short dialogues, for which, once more, there are no accompanying texts in the unit. Although they may not catch every word, they should again listen for the most relevant information. While they are listening, they will have to get certain information from the illustration (places on a map, details in a contract, ticket prices in a concert ad, for example) and apply it to the questions, exercises, or photos *(C)* at the top of the page. Before you start the cassette, present key vocabulary, set the scene, and ask students to think about "who", "what" and "where". You may also want to ask them to listen for differences, for example, in levels of formality between speakers. Then play the recorded conversations one at a time – several times if necessary. Sometimes listening for the gist of the conversation will be enough so that students can do the exercises individually; sometimes they will have to use information from the illustration *(A)*; and sometimes they will have to do both.

D. *Problem solving.* Students' books are open. As they look at the directions and the illustration, prepare the class to work in pairs or small groups. To demonstrate, read one of the tasks and have a student create a free conversation in simple English with you or with another student. Tell the others to do the same. When pairs begin talking, you may want to work with individuals who need extra help. There are no "correct" answers, so this unstructured exercise should be good for shy students.
(You can reverse the order of *D* and *E*, if you wish, or leave *D* for later – after Part III – if it is too difficult for your students at this stage.)

E. Tell students to prepare to work in pairs by putting themselves in the place of the cartoon characters. They should be familiar with the situations by now and be able to remember the conversations from *C* above. Ask students to look at the picture to the right of the speech balloons and make conversations using the pattern and some of the ideas mentioned in the directions. Then ask them to think of situations of their own. They can repeat the pattern many times, using slightly different questions and answers. If necessary, demonstrate the pattern. The thing to keep in mind when doing this exercise is *how to*:

Unit 1: How to ask for and give directions
Unit 2: How to take and leave messages
Unit 3: How to ask for and give detailed information
Unit 4: How to offer help and turn down offers
Unit 5: How to ask to have things done

Unit 6: How to ask and tell how long something will take
Unit 7: How to ask about and describe food
Unit 8: How to talk about your health
Unit 9: How to talk about what there is to do
Unit 10: How to agree to suggestions or get out of something

PART III,
consisting of sections *A* through *E*, presents more language situations and is aimed at expanding the students' skills.

A. *Study the illustration.*
Students open their books and study the illustration individually.

B. *Answer the questions.*
Several students read and answer the comprehension questions and tasks in the middle of the page, or some may be assigned as *homework*. (Optional: Sometimes the realia introduced in *A* and the questions that follow are more important for exploiting new vocabulary than for the particular items of realia themselves. You might wish to use, instead, other realia you have collected. You could assign *A* and *B* as homework, or if you think your students have had enough work with realia, leave these two exercises out.)

C. *Listen and read.*
Students shut their books while you explain that they will be hearing several conversations that they will later be reading. Set the scene and play the first dialogue. Then, as in Part I, students open their books and read along while you play the recording of that dialogue again. Students then listen to and read each of the conversations in the same way.

D. *Answer the questions.*
Although there are several different conversations in *C*, the comprehension questions for all of them are printed as a group following the conversations. Remember to ask the questions about *each* dialogue immediately after *that* dialogue.

E. *Act out the scenes.*
In pairs or small groups, students prepare to read each conversation, each taking a part. They should read the exercises, think about *how* the speakers said certain things, and consciously use these means to act out the scenes in simple English with their partners. By now students should be able to distinguish between various levels of formality. Help them to distinguish, too, between language they should understand but not necessarily use (receptive) and language they should understand and be able to use (productive).

PART IV
consists of a cartoon, sections *A* and *B*, and the glossary.

Cartoon.
Students look at the cartoon at the top of the page. Give them time to think about the situation and figure out what is happening in the cartoon. If someone does not understand the joke, ask another student to try and explain it. Have students tell the joke or story in English in their own words. Then, in English, they can tell other jokes or stories to partners or to the class. You might wish to bring in cartoons and jokes you have collected. The ability to tell jokes in English may well improve the student's ability to get around socially. If students can get a feeling for the American sense of humor, they can get a better sense of the American character and its informality and playfulness.

A. Read the information. Several students read sections of "Here are some more helpful things to know." This concluding text about the general theme of the unit contains additional hints to travelers and newcomers to the U.S. You and your students may have more to add, either in a class discussion or in small groups. This is a good time to encourage students who have traveled in the U.S. to compare their experiences with the customs in their own countries.

B. Compare. (Optional: This section will be useful only to students who have been to Great Britain or have learned some British English. If not, it may just be confusing and should, therefore, be left out.) The vocabulary equivalents can be checked by having students cover one of the columns to see how many words they know and can "translate" from American into British English and vice versa. Explain the differences in pronunciation, meaning, spelling, and usage. Words that are new can be put into contexts by having students make up sentences to illustrate them.

GLOSSARY.
At the end of each unit there is an alphabetical list of important words from that unit. Parts of speech are indicated and definitions are given in simple English. Some words may have more than one meaning, but only meanings from the unit are included. Abbreviations, short forms, and weights and measures that appear in the units are on page 134. Abbreviations of states appear on the U.S. map at the front of the book.
Use the glossary in class for spelling practice. Encourage students to quiz each other on spellings, meanings, and usages of words. Set up a "spelling-bee" with two teams of students competing against each other to earn the highest number of points for the correct spelling of various words you give them from the glossary. Do crossword puzzles with your students or show them how to play spelling boardgames.

PART V
is a review section. The last two pages of each unit consist of consolidation exercises and are designed to be used flexibly, either as homework or as classroom exercises. Show students how to check to see how much they've learned, how to diagnose their own language weaknesses, and how to test themselves so that they can progress on their own.

Review. The realia and the tasks presented at the end of the unit should motivate students to review the completed material, applying what they have learned to one final piece of complicated realia. The tasks should lead students to transfer the skills acquired to their own experience.

Activities. At the top of the last page there are tasks that can be done orally in class or as written homework. Students have to think of definitions and explanations as a form of vocabulary review. The photos can be useful in getting them to talk or write about what they know about the topic in general.
If you or your students have access to American magazines, newspapers, pictures, maps, menus, or other realia, use them to develop strong vocabularies and to make the learning experience more authentic and interesting. Throughout the course, whenever places are mentioned, encourage students to use the map at the front of the book to orient themselves.

Test yourself. This matching test should provide more practice in recognizing register, intonation, accents, and dealing with slang and idiomatic English. While looking at the ten idioms listed on the left, students listen to those same idioms recorded on the cassette and match them with the expression that means the same thing from the list on the right. Some students may be able to do this without the cassette. You can also convert the matching test into a competitive team game.

ANSWERS AND NOTES.
Answers to all the questions and exercises in the book (only examples of *possible* correct answers in some cases), reasons for the answers, and extra information are arranged on pages 107–124 by units. Students can use this to check their homework, or you can use it as an additional teaching aid to expand on answers.

TAPESCRIPT.
Texts to all the recorded conversations in *Listen and answer* and *Look and listen*, those conversations not printed in the units, are arranged on pages 125–133 by units. Students who have the cassette can review by playing the conversations again at home.

ANSWERS AND NOTES

UNIT 1 ✈

Page 2 C

1 The U.S. Immigration and Naturalization Service (INS) does.
2 All non-U.S. citizens who enter the country.
3 In most English-speaking countries, people usually have two given names, a first name and a middle name.
4 Only *you* can answer this one. Your country of residence is the one you live in most of the time, or the one you'll return to when you leave the U.S.

5 The country of citizenship is usually the one where you were born. If you were born in the U.S., you may be able to claim U.S. citizenship.
6 You should keep it with you in your passport. When you leave the country, you should give it to the people working for the airline or ship company. If you go across the border by land, give it to an INS official at the border.

Page 3 D

1 The speakers are a Customs official and a foreigner.
2 They are at a Customs desk.
3 That's his job. He has to make sure people

don't bring anything illegal into the country, and he has to charge a tax (duty) on some things.
5 You can leave the airport.

Page 3 F

1 She's going to go into Manhattan for a few days.
2 He thinks it's a great town. In other words, he likes it a lot.
3 She can take the bus.
4 It's in Manhattan.

5 They leave about every half hour.
6 He's going to fly to L.A. (or Los Angeles).
7 He's going to take the shuttle bus.
8 No, he doesn't think the airport shuttles are cheap, but he doesn't think they are expensive, either.

Page 4 B

1 You take Concourse K. In other words, you walk down the hall marked K to your gate.
2 They are at the far ends of the building. There are two men's and two women's.
3 The restaurant sells food. In the areas marked Concessions there will be some snack bars.
4 Yes, you can. Downstairs near the baggage claim area there are desks marked Budget,

National, Hertz, Dollar, Avis. These are names of some large car rental companies.
5 No, you can take the parking lot shuttle from the lower level. But if you want to walk, there is a special pedestrian tunnel to the parking lots.
6 Yes, it is. There are Tri-Met buses, which are city buses, as well as limousines and taxis.

Page 5 C

1 In the first conversation, they're downstairs near an escalator. The man has to go up the escalator on his left.
2 In the second conversation, they're upstairs to the right of Concourse L. The customer has to

go to his left.
3 In the third conversation, they're upstairs, probably in the middle of the building. The man has to go downstairs.

Page 5 D

1 You can take the escalator to the left and then turn right. You might say, "Excuse me. Can you tell me how to get to the Eastern Airlines counter?" or "Where is the Eastern Airlines counter, please?"

2 "Excuse me, could you tell me where the men's room (or ladies' room or restroom) is?"

Page 6 B

1 The Immigration officer and the Customs inspector.
2 All of them who are travelling with you.

3 If it's over $5,000, you do.

Page 7 D

1 He wants to sit in a window seat in the nonsmoking section.
2 He can't board now because there's a twenty-minute delay.
3 She has to put it on the belt. (It's a moving belt that carries things through an X-ray machine.)
4 Because the airport has to be very sure that no

one is carrying anything dangerous.
5 Because something made the alarm go off, and the officer wants to be sure it was only her bracelet.
6 It tells you to hold the line because all the agents are busy. "Hold the line" means "wait."

Page 10

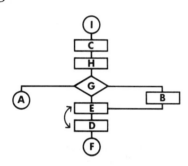

1 Note: No two airports are exactly the same. At some, you may check in at the gate where you board the plane, which means that D may come before E.
2 The places marked on the Boston airport map are Pier B, U.S. Customs Inspection, Baggage Claim Area, and U.S. Immigration.

Page 11 Activities

Newsstand: to buy magazines and newspapers; *lost and found:* to turn in something they found or to ask about something they lost; *currency exchange:* to exchange money; *restrooms:* to go to the bathroom or wash their faces or hands; *nursery:* to take care of their babies – change their

diapers or nurse them; *concessions:* to get something they can eat standing up (a snack); *travel insurance:* to buy travel insurance; *post office:* to buy stamps or mail letters; *car rentals:* to rent a car.

Test yourself

1 i; 2 h & i; 3 f; 4 g; 5 c; 6 h & d; 7 b; 8 e; 9 g; 10 a.
Yes: 1 and 2; No: 3; To respond to Thanks: 1, 2,

4, 9 and, of course, "You're welcome." To attract attention: 5.

UNIT 2 📞

Page 12 C

1 It costs 25¢. Yes, that is two dimes and a nickel. (The cost varies in different parts of the U.S. A call may cost 10¢, 15¢, 20¢ or 25¢.)
2 No, it will only take U.S. coins.
3 Yes, you can. You can press the coin release lever. (You can also hang up, and your money will come back.)
4 Dial 0. (In some cities, dial 911 – pay phones will always tell you which number to call.)

For information, look in the phone book or dial 1-555-1212.
5 Yes, you can, if it's a station-to-station call.
6 Dial 1-206 and then the number. A computer voice or operator will tell you how much money to deposit.
7 No, you don't. In an emergency, you can call the police or a doctor through the operator and you don't have to pay.

Page 13   D

1 Vic is in all three conversations. In the first one, he's talking to a Directory Assistance (or information) operator. In the second one, he's talking to an operator. In the third one, he's talking to his friend Henry. The operator only interrupts to ask him to put $3.00 into the slot.
2 He's calling from Baton Rouge.
3 He's calling from a public (or pay) phone.
4 Henry's number had been changed.
5 You would need nickels (5¢ coins), dimes (10¢ coins), and quarters (25¢ coins).
6 The best thing to do is ask someone where there's a phone booth. You can also look in a shopping center, gas station, or restaurant.

Page 13   F

1 He can buy them from a machine.
2 He needs a telephone.
3 Near the information desk. The sign "Phone" is often in blue and white.
4 He'll need some change.
5 Yes, it is.
6 He'll probably go the the bank and get change.
7 This attendant is perhaps a little bit too friendly. Many Americans like to talk – to tell about themselves and to ask other people about themselves.

Page 14   B

1 A dial-direct call is the cheapest.
2 A person-to-person call is the most expensive.
3 You get the largest discount after 11 p.m. at night and on weekends.
4 The operator has to help you with person-to-person, collect, Calling Card, coin, billed to a third number, hotel guest, and time and charge calls.
5 You have to pay for at least one minute.
6 You have to pay for at least one minute.
7 No. The charge is based on distance and is in addition to dial-direct rates.
8 It costs you $3.38 for the first minute and 26 ¢ for each additional minute. (These rates are for 1983.)
9 It would have cost you 38 ¢ for the first minute and 26 ¢ for each minute after that.

Page 15   C

1 In the first conversation, a woman talks to a Directory Assistance operator and then to an operator. She obviously doesn't know them.
2 In the second conversation, a woman is talking to Terry, who works at a travel agency. They don't know each other. The message would be, "Sherry Snyder of Standard Oil called from Dallas. She'll try to call again."
3 In the third conversation, a young man is calling his friend and talks to his friend's mother. They know each other and are casual with each other on the phone. The message would be, "Wally called about tennis tomorrow. Call him back this evening."
4 The message on the answering machine is casual and is for Jean's friends. Your message should give your name, the time when you called, your number, and when Jean can reach you.

Page 16   B

1 The name, address and telephone number of the person receiving the telegram, and the name, address and phone number of the sender. You also need to check the box in the upper right-hand corner if you want the telegram sent overnight. (That's cheaper.)
2 Valerie Olson is sending this telegram. She writes that she will be arriving by train at twenty minutes past eight in the evening on January 8th.
3 The person receiving the telegram (the recipient) is Jerry Sapier. He doesn't have his own address. He is staying with Pat McLaughlin in Indianapolis.
4 Yes, she is. She writes "Can't wait," which means that she is very excited and can hardly wait to get there.
5 Telegram style leaves out lots of unimportant words, like "I," "the," "a," "on," "at" and so on. Here is a sample message: "Arriving Monday 10:15 a.m. bus from Hartford stop please meet stop".

Page 17 D

1 Because the postmaster doesn't know him and he has to be sure he is giving mail to the right person.
2 Surface mail goes on land or sea; air mail goes in planes; express mail is handled specially and should take less time to arrive; registered mail has a special number on it so the post office can find (or trace) it if it doesn't arrive.
3 Because the package has to arrive as soon as possible.

Page 20

1 First, find the area code using the area code map. Then pick up the receiver and dial the number. When the voice tells you how much money the call will cost, put your coins in the slot.
2 It's 404.
3 It would be cheapest at night or on weekends. You could talk ten minutes for under $2.00.
4 You could send a telegram or write a letter.

Page 21 Activities

The *white pages* contain all telephone numbers but no advertising; the *Yellow Pages* contain the numbers of businesses and advertising for them. *Area codes* are three-digit numbers in the telephone system; *zip codes* are five-digit numbers (this will eventually change to nine digits) used by the postal system. *Station-to-station* and *person-to-person* are types of long distance phone calls. The first one means that the caller will talk to anyone who answers; the second one means that the caller will pay only if he speaks to the person he asks for.
Airmail is mail that goes by plane; *surface mail* goes by ship, truck or train.
A *dime* is a coin worth 10¢; a *quarter* is worth 25¢.
A *packet* is a package that weighs two pounds or less; a *parcel* weighs more.
An *operator-assisted* call is one the operator helps you with; a *dial-direct* call is one you can make without talking to the operator. *Express* mail is handled specially – it's very fast but expensive; *registered* mail is recorded by the post office so they can trace it (follow its route) if it doesn't arrive.

Test yourself

1 d; 2 g; 3 f; 4 e; 5 h; 6 a; 7 i; 8 j; 9 c; 10 b.

You or an operator might use these in a conversation: 2, 5, 6 and 8.

UNIT 3

Page 22 C

1 From Ugly Duckling.
2 Some others are Avis, Budget, Dollar, Thrifty, National and Rent-A-Junker.
3 Avis, Budget, Hertz, Dollar, Thrifty and National rent new cars.
4 The weekly rate is cheaper if you'll be driving more than 140 miles.
5 Yes, they do. They will credit you half the cost of your gas.
6 The daily rate applies, and you have to pay 10¢ per mile.
7 Yes, because the weekly rate includes only 500 miles.
8 No, they don't.
9 You can take their shuttle from the airport. (You have to call them and request it.)

Page 23 D

1 The rental agent and Ms. Ferris.
2 She wanted to rent a smaller car than the one she reserved.
3 She'll return it on Friday.
4 She charges it; that is, she uses her Visa (credit) card to pay for it.
5 Some things to consider are: how much room you need, the car's gas mileage, how many miles you'll probably drive, how long you'll need the car.
6 The best thing to do is ask the rental agent.

Page 23 F

1 He reserved a Ford Granada.
2 It includes liability and $350 deductible collision.
3 It means the insurance company pays damages over $350 if they result from an accident. The $5 a day eliminates the deductible; that is, if you pay it, you won't have to pay any of the damages that might result from a collision.
4 Personal accident covers medical bills from an accident – here, the first $2,000 would be paid.
5 Yes, he does. He wants the collision damage waiver, but not personal accident.
6 She asks him to sign it.

Page 24 B

1 The rate per mile is $0.34 and per day it's $29.
2 Yes, it allows him 300 miles.
3 It was three-quarters full when he picked it up and one-quarter full when he brought it back.
4 No, he didn't.
5 No, he didn't.
6 He should give it to the car rental company with the money to pay it.
7 The lessor is the car rental company.
8 Mr. Taylor and anybody who has the company's written permission.
9 Mr. Taylor lets the company charge the cost of renting the car to his credit card. He agrees not to let other people drive the car unless they get permission from the company first. He says he has read all the terms on both sides of the agreement, and understands and agrees with them.

Page 25 C

1 If the car breaks down, the customer should call the number the agent gives him. The people he calls will see that he gets help.
2 You can check either the box marked "declines CDW" or the one marked "accepts CDW," and either the box marked "declines PAI" or the one marked "accepts PAI." CDW means collision damage waiver and PAI means personal accident insurance.
3 If there's an accident, you have to notify the police and fill out one of the car rental company's accident reports. If you get a parking ticket, you have to turn it in with the money to pay it when you return the car.

Page 26 B

1 headlights; 2 windshield wipers; 3 gas tank; 4 foot brake; 5 parking brake; 6 turn signals (these are also called "blinkers"); 7 fenders; 8 trunk; 9 tail lights; 10 rearview mirror; 11 hood; 12 horn; 13 gearshift lever; 14 steering wheel.

Page 27 D

1 He puts $10 worth of unleaded gas in the tank, checks the oil, and washes the windshield.
2 It's very good.
3 Fill the tank with regular and check the tires.
4 He does the first but not the second, because it's a mini-serve island.
5 It seems to be Hank's fault.
6 Hank's car's fender was damaged. The whole side of Bill's car was scratched.
7 Linda wants them to move their cars out of the way. Bill wants her to give him her address because he thinks she saw the accident.

Page 30

1 #1 was going south on DeMont.
2 #2 intended to turn left.
3 I was going south on DeMont. In the middle of the intersection with S. 14th, another car suddenly turned in front of me. The driver didn't signal first. I hit the car and we both ended up on S. 14th.
4 One other vehicle; remain stopped in traffic; passenger car; raining, wet; daylight.

Page 31 Activities

Liability insurance pays for injuries and damages, to other people and their property; *personal accident insurance* pays for your own medical bills if you have an accident. *Cash* and *charge* are two ways of paying. *Cash* means you pay with cash (coins and bills) or by check, and *charge* means you give the agent your credit card and promise to pay later. A *deposit* is money you give to someone to keep while you are using something of theirs; a *refund* is money you get back when you have paid too much. A *ticket* is a notice of arrest for a traffic violation. A *summons* is a demand that you come to court; all tickets are summonses, but people usually call them tickets. *Coverage* is the amount of damage an insurance company will cover or pay for; *deductible* is the amount of damage a customer must pay. *Mileage* is the number of miles a car has been driven, or the number of miles per gallon it gets; *mph* stands for miles per hour. *Regular, unleaded* and *premium* are types of gas. *Unleaded* has no lead in it; *regular* is cheaper but it doesn't have as much power; *premium* is for sports cars and others with high-performance engines. *Mini-serve, full-serve* and *self-serve* are types of gas station islands. At the *mini-serve* island, attendants will only put gas in your car. At the *full-serve*, they will check your

oil, tires, etc. At the *self-serve*, you put the gas in the tank. *Fenders* are on the sides of the car over the tires; *bumpers* are in the front and back of the car. They lessen the force of a bump or shock to the car. In the U.S. drivers sometimes use their bumpers while parking. *Turn signals* are lights that show you're going to turn; *tail lights* are red lights on the back of the car; *headlights* are bright, white lights on the front of the car. You push the *foot brake* with your foot to stop the car; you set the *parking brake* by hand before you get out of your car. It stops the car from rolling. The *trunk* is for storing or carrying large things, and it's usually at the back of the car; the *hood* covers the engine. A person is *injured*, and property is *damaged*.

Test yourself

1 f; 2 j; 3 g; 4 a; 5 h; 6 b; 7 d; 8 i; 9 c; 10 e.
These probably sound friendly: 5, 7 and 8.
These probably sound angry: 2, 4, 6 and 10.

Number 3 can be either – it depends on the situation. In this unit, it sounds angry. Polite ones are: 1 and 9.

UNIT 4

Page 32 C

1 They operate 24 hours a day.
2 The cabs have meters.
3 Yes, you can. ("air-conditioned tours")
4 Yes, they do. ("ask about discount rates")
5 Yes, you can. ("deliveries")

6 Yes, you can. ("jumper service")
7 Yes, they might. ("business accounts"; this means you can charge taxi expenses to your company.)
8 Yes, they do – Visa and Master Charge.

Page 33 D

1 The speakers are: a bus driver and two passengers on the bus; a cab driver and a customer.
2 They are on a bus and in a cab.
3 One passenger doesn't have exact change to pay the bus fare.

4 You can take city buses or taxis, or you can drive. In some cities you can take the subway, too.
5 From city to city: train (sometimes), bus, and plane.

Page 33 F

1 She wants to go to Chicago.
2 There are two per day.
3 The Broadway via Pittsburgh is faster.
4 Yes, you can eat in dining rooms or snack

bars on the trains.
5 Yes, you can, in roomettes or slumber coaches.
6 No, she hasn't.

Page 34 B

1 a.m. times are lighter than p.m. times.
2 The short forms are "Lv" and "Ar."
3 # means "rest stop." In other words, you can get out of the bus and go to the bathroom.
4 MT means Mountain Time and PT means Pacific Time.

5 Yes, you do. You have to change in Sacramento.
6 Bus 6223 runs between Salt Lake and San Francisco.
7 It leaves Oakland at 11:20 a.m. Pacific Time and arrives in Salt Lake at 5:10 a.m. Mountain Time.

Page 35 C

1 It will stop for a meal in Lovelock, Nevada, at 6:55 p.m.
2 It goes to Chicago. It takes two and a half days.
3 This happens because of a time zone change

from Pacific to Mountain Time. It really takes an hour and ten minutes.
4 They go through California, Nevada, Utah, Colorado, Nebraska, Iowa and Illinois.

Page 36 B

1 No, trips outside New York City cost more.
2 No, they don't.
3 You can call the Port Authority Police or see

the taxi dispatcher.
4 From 10:15 a.m. to 2:15 a.m.

Page 37 D

1 He has to go to the far side of town and then follow the signs.
2 He has to buy his ticket at least two weeks in

advance and stay at least eight days. Yes, he qualifies.

Page 41 Activities

cab: taxi; *coach*: a comfortable bus or car on a train; *depot*: station; *buck*: dollar; *schedule*: timetable; *rapid transit*: subway.

A *round trip* ticket is one that takes you to a place and back again; a *one way* ticket just takes you to the place. A *subway* is a train that travels under the ground; an *el* (short for "elevated") is a train that's raised above the street. A bus or train *picks up* passengers when it stops to let them get on; it *discharges* passengers when it stops to let them get off. A *slumber coach* on a train sleeps two people;

so does a *roomette*, but it has a wash basin and a toilet, too. The hours from midnight to noon (midday) are *a.m.*; the hours from noon to midnight are *p.m. PT* means Pacific Time; *MT* means Mountain Time; *CT* means Central Time; *ET* means Eastern Time. When they are abbreviated with an S, as in *MST*, it means Mountain Standard Time. *D* means Daylight Time, which is in effect from the last weekend in April until the last weekend in October.

Test yourself

1 a; 2 e; 3 f; 4 g; 5 h; 6 c; 7 b; 8 a; 9 d; 10 a.
For something that'll happen quickly: 1, 8 and 10,

and, of course, "In a moment." To turn down help politely: 3.

UNIT 5

Page 42 C

1 The Caravan is definitely open – the ad says "24 hour desk service."
2 The Flamingo has a swimming pool, but the Caravan would be better for other things because it's next ("adjacent") to a 12-acre park and the new YMCA.
3 The Caravan is downtown, so you'll probably pick it.
4 The Flamingo is closer to the airport.
5 It's the Flamingo, which belongs to the Best Western Motel chain.

Page 43 D

1 They are clerks at the two motels.
2 He's calling from a phone booth.
3 He wants a double room.
4 He wants a room with a waterbed.
5 They are hotels, motels, lodges, inns, resorts, and camping grounds.
6 Yes, you can.
7 Most hotels and motels have special facilities (family units, bridal suites, swimming pools, saunas, convention aids, meeting rooms). Ask about them when you arrive or when you make your reservation.

Page 43 F

1 It's over twenty feet square. It's a double, and it has a refrigerator.
2 No, there isn't.
3 They don't rent a suite because it would be very expensive, and because the double room is large enough for them.
4 They have to pay in advance because they are paying cash.
5 The clerk wants his name, address, and the make and license number of his car.
6 They have to check out by noon.
7 The bellman, Harvey, will show them to their room.
8 It's 615.
9 He pays cash – in travelers checks.
10 They should let the clerk know – call her or tell her in person.

Page 44 B

1 Its name is Majestic Cleaners.
2 No, it isn't. It's on Sandy Boulevard.
3 No, it doesn't.
4 No, they aren't.
5 You'd mark "Suits, men's (2 pc)" and "Vests." Write the number of suits you want cleaned in the first column on the left under "No."
6 It costs $9.25 for a man's three-piece suit.
7 Can you find them? All of the prices that have "up" after them can be higher than the price listed here. The others are firm or fixed.

Page 45 C

1 Put a "1" in front of man's suit, etc. Your cleaning bill would be $7.50 for the man's suit, $7.50 or more for the lady's suit, $2.00 or more for the necktie, $8.00 or more for two pairs of pants. That would come to at least $25.00.
2 Well, how much would it be for you?
3 The line is at the bottom of the form. It says, "Prices subject to change without notice."
4 You should say something like, "Please dry-clean this shirt. Do not press it with steam."

Page 46 B

1 They want to know how to serve their customers better, so they want to know what you liked and didn't like.
2 You should return it to the front desk or mail it to the hotel.

Page 47 D

1 He asked the hotel clerk to have the bathroom light looked at and a room service menu brought to his room.
2 They ask for advice on where to shop for certain things.
3 She tells them about a department store, two shoe stores, a cookware shop, a bookstore and an import store. She also suggests Beaverton Mall, a shopping center about five miles away.

Page 50

1 The Hartley Inn.
2 It's a chain hotel owned by Hartley Hotels and Motor Inns.
3 It has 200 of them.
4 It has two – the Polo Restaurant, which sounds more expensive, and the Scandia Café, which sounds more casual.
5 Yes, it does. It has games and sports (tennis courts, a swimming pool, putting green, etc.).
6 Yes, it does. It has 4,700 square feet (that's about 520 square meters) of meeting, banquet and convention space.
7 There's a gift shop and an Eastern Airlines ticket desk.
8 It provides airport limousines and a valet – a person who will pick up and return your rented car or your own car, if it has to be repaired.
9 Business people. Most of the special services and facilities they list are ones business people would like to use, such as the UPI news machine.
10 It has a barber shop and a special Decathlon Health Club for men only. Probably there are more men than women who stay at this hotel. Why? Probably because there are no special facilities for women, although there are several for men, including the Games Room – with "masculine decor."

Page 51 Activities

Desk clerks make reservations, check people in and out of the hotel, take care of keys, and handle problems. *Switchboard operators* answer the phone and transfer calls to the people who are being called. *Room service waiters* take orders for food and drinks in people's rooms, bring the orders and sometimes take the dirty dishes away. *Maids* clean the rooms and change the sheets. A *bellman* carries hotel guests' bags to their rooms.

The *front desk* is where you find the desk clerk. People go there to check in or out, to turn in or pick up their keys, their mail and messages, or to complain about something in the hotel. *Lobbies* are big, open rooms near the front desk. Usually people go there to meet friends. *Lounges* are

comfortable bars. People go there to have a drink and relax. *Suites* are groups of rooms – usually a bedroom and living room, sometimes with a kitchen – that you can rent in a hotel. *Meeting rooms* are for meetings. People rent them to meet with other people or talk about business when they don't want to do it in their rooms. *Game rooms* have games like pool, billiards, backgammon, chess, etc., in them. People go there to play these games and relax. *Gift shops* have souvenirs, books, cards and other similar items. *Piano bars* are bars built around pianos. People can sit very close to the piano and listen to the music.

Test yourself

1 c & h; 2 g; 3 f; 4 b & i; 5 c & h; 6 d; 7 a; 8 j; 9 e; 10 b & i.

Something's broken: 1 and 5, c and h.
To ask someone to repair it: 4 and 10, b and i.

UNIT 6

Page 52 C

1 It has longer hours than most banks; the ad says "extended banking hours."
2 The hours range from 7:00 a.m. to 8:00 p.m. Yes, they are unusually long.
3 It has three branches.
4 Western Bank sells travelers checks.
5 First Interstate does.
6 Yes, it is. An international credit card is the best kind to have.
7 The best way to carry cash is in travelers checks.
8 Travelers checks should be in dollars if you're traveling in the U.S. It isn't convenient to have them in any other currency because they are harder to cash.
9 The best place is the main office of a bank in a city.
10 Yes, you can.

Page 53 D

1 The speakers are a bank teller and a customer.
2 He wants travelers checks.
3 He wants to pay by Eurocheque.
4 You have to show some ID, like your passport.
5 Go to an office of the company you bought them from. If they were stolen, you should also tell the police.

Page 53 F

1 He lost his travelers checks.
2 He wanted them to replace his checks.
3 He had to call an office in New York.
4 No, because it was a toll-free number.
5 How much he'd lost, what the check numbers were, where he bought the checks and if he had any ID.
6 It was fairly easy because he knew the numbers of the checks he lost. It would have been more difficult if he hadn't had the numbers.

Page 54 B

1 Arthur Sutton is.
2 His address is 8263 E. 183rd., Cleveland, Ohio 44119, and his phone number is 481-6772.

3 The recipient's name is James Sutton.
4 His address is 4303 Spruce St., Albuquerque, New Mexico 87106, and his phone number is 387-8333.
5 Three hundred dollars is being cabled to him.
6 His message is, "Hope this helps get your car fixed."
7 The question is, "What's wrong with your car?"

8 There's some important information there, probably the terms the sender agrees to when he signs the money order.
9 You can send or "file" your money order by phone.
10 You can send up to $300 this way.

Page 56 B

1 So they can check on you and see if you are a good credit risk (that is, responsible enough for them to loan money to) before they give you credit.
2 Your name, your present and former addresses, a lot of information about your

family and your past and present jobs, some personal references, your Social Security number, and your credit history.
3 So they can use them to establish a credit rating for you – that is, to decide how much money they will let you borrow.

Page 57 D

1 She has thirty days to exchange things, but she has to keep the receipt, which is the same as the sales slip.
2 He wanted to know how long the guarantee was for.

3 His girlfriend had the travelers checks, and the store wouldn't accept his out-of-state personal check.
4 Yes, they will.

Page 60

1 You have to give them your Social Security number, your name and home address, your signature, your occupation, your birth date, the names of your parents and your wife or husband (spouse), and her or his occupation.
2 You would write the date. On the right in the box next to "Currency," you would write

$200.00. Then you list the checks by bank number – this is the number in small print in the upper right-hand corner. Here it is 24-12/1230. At the bottom, you write the total of cash and checks you want to put in your account.

Page 61 Activities

A *personal check* is written against your bank account; a *travelers check* is purchased from a bank and insured. *Cash* and *charge* are ways of paying; *cash* is with cash or check, *charge* is with a credit card. A *service charge* is a fee (money) you pay once when a person or company does something for you; *interest* is the price you pay for using somebody else's money. To *sign* means to write your signature on something; to *countersign* means to sign a second time; to *initial* means to sign your initials. *Layaway* is when you agree to buy something by putting a few dollars down and paying the rest of the price later; you don't take the item home until you've paid, and the store charges no interest; the *installment plan* allows the customer to make a down payment, take the item home, and pay money every month (installments). You also pay interest. Installments are usually for expensive things, while layaway is usually for inexpensive things (especially clothes). A *gift certificate* is a paper you buy from a store as

a present. The person you give it to can spend it like money at that store. A *warranty* is a paper that tells what the maker of a product will do to repair or replace it and for how long. The *sender* sends something to a *recipient*, the person who receives the thing. A *telegram* is a message sent over wires, written down when it arrives, and delivered by phone or mail. A *night letter* is a telegram sent at night and delivered by mail the following day. A *telegraphic money order* is an order to pay money sent by telegram. A *personal reference* is someone who knows you well and will tell other people (an employer, a bank, etc.) about you, especially good things; an *employer* is the person or company you work for. To *make out a check* means that you fill it out in writing and make it payable to someone, writing their name on the line after "Pay to the order of." To *take a personal check* means that a store, hotel or other organization will accept your personal check as payment.

Test yourself

1 h; 2 a; 3 e; 4 g; 5 b; 6 j; 7 i; 8 d; 9 c; 10 f.

When shopping: 3, 6, 7 and 8.
When doing other business: 1, 2, 4, 5, 7, 9 and 10.

UNIT 7

Page 62   C

1 Clockwise from upper left the names are the Golden Dragon, Shakey's Pizza Parlor, the Pancake Pantry, and Le Cuisinier.
2 Clockwise from upper left, they serve Chinese food; pizza, chicken, and sandwiches; pancakes; and French food.
3 The Golden Dragon is open from 11:30 a.m. to 3:00 a.m.; Shakey's ad doesn't say; the Pancake Pantry is open 24 hours a day; and Le Cuisinier is open from 6:00 to 10:00 p.m. Tuesday through Saturday, and for Sunday brunch at 10:00.
4 The Golden Dragon and Shakey's probably serve lunch and dinner; the Pancake Pantry serves breakfast, lunch and dinner; Le Cuisinier serves dinner and also serves brunch once a week.

5 The Golden Dragon has a lounge, so it serves alcohol; Shakey's and the Pancake Pantry probably don't, as nothing in their ads suggests it; Le Cuisinier probably serves wine because it features "fine French dining," and that includes wine.
6 The pancake house serves lunch and dinner anytime.
7 You can get food "to go" at the Golden Dragon or Shakey's. (This ad calls it "carryout.")
8 Le Cuisinier is the most expensive and also the dressiest. How can you tell from the ad? Clues are "fine," "French," "reservations," and the picture in the ad. The most casual is probably Shakey's. Pizza parlors are usually very casual in the U.S.

Page 63   D

1 A man who works at the restaurant answers the phone. Mr. Novak wants a reservation for next Saturday night.
2 He reserves for 8:00.
3 They are probably walking into the foyer or entrance area of a medium-priced, semi-dressy restaurant.
4 They don't sit down right away because the

sign says to wait to be seated.
5 Because she says she's allergic to smoke.
6 Yes, he does. But he isn't very polite about it. When he says "You win, lady," he really means "Okay, I'll do what you say, but only because you insist."
7 You order after you've gotten a table and the waiter or waitress comes to take your order.

Page 63   F

1 She wants a cup of coffee with cream.
2 George is going to pay.
3 Rice and barbecued tomatoes come with the beef-kabob.

4 Tossed green salad and chips come with the French dip.
5 Turkey, bacon, lettuce, sliced tomato and cheddar cheese are in a club sandwich.

Page 64   B

1 They're open from 5:30 to 10:30 p.m. Tuesday through Saturday.
2 They make fresh soups in the restaurant.
3 Can you? You might say something like this: A shrimp louie is a house salad (that is, a green salad with tomato and alfalfa sprouts) with shrimp in it. A chef's salad is a tossed green salad with meat and cheese slices in it.
4 You eat hors d'oeuvres before the main part of the dinner.

5 Salad, a vegetable, an Idaho potato and bread come with the dinners.
6 Prawns Orientale comes with rice instead of potatoes.
7 They always serve lemon cheesecake and buttermilk chocolate cake, and they serve three or four others that change each day.
8 Ask your waiter if you want to find out about the desserts.
9 You can read the wine list or ask.

Page 65   C

1 You might say, "If I order the prime rib, could I substitute rice for potatoes?"
2 Only the top sirloin and the prime rib are definitely beef; spareribs can be either, but are usually pork. Ask your waiter if you want to know for sure.
3 You shouldn't order spareribs unless you ask the waiter about them, or chicken livers in

bacon or the Chef's Salad (ham).
4 If you make a reservation, you could ask for a quiet table. If you don't, you'd just ask for a table for two when you get to the restaurant. You'd probably suggest hors d'oeuvres, one of the most expensive dinners, and a very good wine.

Page 66 B

1 It'll cost you $5.59. After that you'll have to pay $7.99 per can. (Although the ad uses the word "tin," most Americans use "can" whether they're talking or writing.)

2 There are three kinds: freeze-dried, ground, and instant. Ground coffee comes in two different grinds: regular and drip, for drip coffee makers. Ground Sanka costs $6.99/2 lb (or 32 oz), which is slightly less expensive than MJB at $5.99/26 oz.

3 One box is 33¢; the ad says "three for 99¢."

4 Can you list them? Give the prices, too.

Page 67 D

1 He adds baked beans, coffee, and popcorn.

2 They decide not to buy any TV dinners.

3 It's Sunday morning.

4 Melinda gives the clerk $55.

5 She gets $1.60 in change.

Page 70

1 Look in the second column under "Type of food" to find the answer.

2 Look under "Hours" in the third column to see if the restaurants serve lunch.

3 Look under "Remarks" in the last column. The Parker House requires jackets.

4 See "Remarks." You could take people in wheelchairs to The Parker House and Iruna Restaurant. They could try the other restaurants, too, but there might not be room for a wheelchair at the table or in the restroom and it might involve steps to climb. You can take children to any of these restaurants, but they'd probably feel particularly at home at the English Room.

5 Only you can decide this! Look under "Prices" and "Credit cards," columns 4 and 5, to choose the moderately priced ones.

Page 71 Activities

Breakfast is the first meal of the day; *brunch* is a late breakfast with breakfast and lunch dishes; *lunch* is the noon meal, usually smaller than dinner and often eaten quickly; *supper* is a light evening meal; *dinner* is an evening or large noon meal. (Many people always say either "dinner" or "supper" to mean their evening meal. Then there's no difference between the two.) *Raw* means not cooked at all; *well-done* means cooked completely. These words can be used for meat or vegetables or fish, while the other words here are only for meat. *Rare* means just cooked a little bit; *medium* means the meat is pink inside; *medium-rare* is between medium and rare. *Soft drinks* are sweet, carbonated drinks without any alcohol; *hard drinks* are made with liquor: vodka, bourbon, gin, tequila, etc. Beer and wine are not usually considered to be hard drinks. *Straight* and *on the rocks* are ways of serving liquor. *Straight* means straight out of the bottle, not mixed with anything; *on the rocks* means with ice cubes. You order food *to go* when you want to take it somewhere to eat it. You get a *doggie bag* when a restaurant meal is too big for you to finish there and you want to take the rest home with you.

A *sandwich shop* makes sandwiches and probably sells soft drinks, potato chips, and some desserts. A *deli* sells cheeses, cooked meats and prepared salads, and will also make sandwiches. A *fast food drive-in* sells "fast food" – hamburgers, tacos, hot dogs, etc. A *cafeteria* sells prepared meals that are cooked in advance – the food may be overcooked. A *coffee shop* will have coffee and desserts as well as small meals. A *cosmopolitan American restaurant* will probably serve nice meals, often from a variety of countries.

Test yourself

1 b; 2 e; 3 b; 4 f; 5 d; 6 a; 7 h; 8 i; 9 g; 10 c.

To invite someone to be your guest: 1 and 3. To ask about dishes: 4.

UNIT 8

Page 72 C

1 There are special directions for children on the lower right-hand side.
2 You can take up to 12 tablets a day, according to the directions.
3 You should take one or two at a time.
4 Yes, it can.

5 The directions claim that it will.
6 The directions claim that it will.
7 Probably not. The directions don't say anything about taking aspirin for diarrhea.
8 Look at the directions to check your list.

Page 73 D

1 The woman is getting a cold or the flu; the first man has a sore throat; the second man, who's talking to a nurse, has hay fever.
2 She's going to stay in bed and drink something hot.

3 He's talking to a doctor.
4 He wants a prescription for hay fever medicine.
5 You call or go to the doctor's office and ask for an appointment.

Page 73 F

1 She wants to see the doctor as soon as possible.
2 Yes, she is. She's never been to this doctor before.
3 She's dizzy and she has bad diarrhea.
4 She wants her to come in at 3:00 that afternoon.

5 The office call will cost $55.
6 No, she isn't.
7 It's Evanston, Illinois.
8 She'll pay the bill right after she sees the doctor today. Because Sheila doesn't live in the same town as the doctor, they want their money before she leaves.

Page 74 B

1 She's female.
2 No, she doesn't.
3 No, she isn't.
4 She's had one. It was in November, 1976.
5 She's had migraine headaches, kidney or

bladder problems, and a miscarriage.
6 Probably varicose veins and heart attacks run in her family.
7 Her grandmother died of TB.
8 Yes, she's had two.

Page 76 B

1 If the employee gets a salary (fixed payment at regular intervals), coverage goes into effect on the first day of work. Employees that get a wage (payment by the hour) are covered after 90 days on the job.
2 You enroll by filling out the enrollment card

within 31 days after you become eligible to enroll.
3 Yes, you do.
4 You file your claims when you have collected a few doctor bills, or within 90 days after the calendar year ends.

Page 77 D

1 Because she hurt her wrist.
2 Yes, he does. (He says, "Okay, take these.")
3 He's got diarrhea and he's been throwing up.

4 Yes, it *could* have been, although he says he probably didn't eat anything that was spoiled.

Page 80

1 You could have a baby delivered wherever there are obstetric (or OB) services. Provident Hospital has OB/GYN and Johns Hopkins has the Woman's Clinic.
2 The U.S. Public Health Service Hospital doesn't treat children (no pediatric services); neither does Good Samaritan (core services, except pediatrics).
3 Johns Hopkins is. It has 1,136 beds.

4 Neither JFK Institute for Handicapped Children nor has Good Samaritan emergency services.
5 The U.S. Public Health Service Hospital does. It has a Center for Occupational and Environmental Health.
6 Provident Hospital is probably the best. See the section that begins "Infectious Diseases."

Page 81 Activities

These are the symptoms: *a cold:* runny or stuffy nose, sneezing, sometimes sore throat, headache, low energy, plugged-up ears; *food poisoning:* diarrhea and nausea, sometimes vomiting and stomach cramps, sometimes fever; *hay fever:* swollen, itchy and runny eyes, sneezing, stuffy nose, sometimes a tight or swollen throat or a cough; *appendicitis:* severe stomachache or pains, sore abdomen; *the flu:* aching muscles, headache, upset stomach and vomiting and/or diarrhea; *a sprain:* swelling and pain in a joint after an accident.

X-rays are pictures of the bones taken through the flesh; *throat cultures* are samples of germs from the throat that are then grown in the laboratory. *Swollen* means larger than usual in size; a leg or arm is *broken* when the bone is broken; it's *sprained* when the muscles and ligaments have been badly twisted. Your *wrist* is the joint between your arm and your hand; your *ankle* is the joint between your leg and your foot. A *disease* is when your body isn't working properly because of germs; a *disorder* is when it isn't working properly because of a physical or mechanical problem.

Test yourself

1 d; 2 f; 3 h; 4 i; 5 g; 6 a; 7 e; 8 j; 9 c; 10 b.
To talk about getting sick: 6 and 10; a and b.

To talk about being sick: 2, 3, 8 and 10; b, f and h.

UNIT 9

Page 82 C

1 Movies are in the *Voice* on page 64 and in the *Times* in Section 2, page 19. Plays On and Off Broadway are in the *Voice* on page 110 and in the *Times* in Section 2, pages 1, 4 and 6.
2 You should look under Dance Events on page 98.
3 The *Voice* doesn't, but the *Times* has one in Section 2, pages 1, 33 and 33B.
4 In the *Voice* on page 114 and probably in the *Times*, Section 1, under Amusements.
5 Yes. In the *Voice* it's on page 101, but also under Galleries on page 122. In the *Times* it's in Section 2, page 29. You could look under Photography, too.

Page 83 D

1 They're in New York City.
2 They can't decide whether to see a play, a musical, or a movie.
3 They're going to look in the newspaper, and then Greg is going to call some box offices to see about tickets.
4 In the daily or weekly newspaper, in *TV Guide*, or in the cable TV guide.

Page 83 F

1 He thinks it's a stupid show.
2 He says "Not bad," so he probably thinks it's okay.
3 He'd like to watch a documentary about Africa or wild animals or something like that.
4 He thinks he and Marge are too old for it. (Walt Disney's shows are usually for children.)
5 He doesn't know anything at all about it, but he thinks it probably isn't.
6 No, they don't.
7 They find something in the cable guide part of the listings.
8 They decide to watch it because they've heard it's a good movie. ("That's supposed to be" means "people say it is.")

Page 84 B

1 The rock concerts are at the Capitol Theater; Keith Jarrett is at Avery Fisher Hall; and the *Messiah* is at Avery Fisher and Carnegie Halls.
2 You can go to the box office at Avery Fisher Hall or to a Ticketron center, you can charge your tickets by calling Centercharge, or you can order them by mail.
3 No, you can't. You can get them by mail, or you can call the number listed in the ad.
4 You make your check out to Masterwork. You have to send a stamped, self-addressed envelope (SASE).

5 The conductor is David Randolph.
6 It's open Monday through Friday from 12:00 to 9:00p.m. and Saturday from 12:00 to 5:00 p.m.
7 You can call one of the two phone numbers listed in the ad.
8 No, the Rossington Collins Band and the Police concerts are sold out.
9 No, you can't. The ad says, "No cans or bottles allowed."

Page 85 C

1 You could choose from the lower-priced seats at both concert halls.
2 You could see Dire Straits or Rockpile and Moon Martin.

3 You can call the number listed at Centercharge and charge the tickets over the phone.

Page 86 B

1 It's for the Seattle Opera Guild's Pub Jump. Anyone over 21 can go.
2 The Seattle Opera Guild is putting it on. A radio station, KOMO, and *The Weekly*, a Seattle paper, are helping (supporting) it.
3 You can get tickets at The Ticket Place, and at the Bon Downtown Store, plus all its suburban outlets, or you can call one of the phone numbers listed or you can order the tickets by mail.

4 It's never a good idea to send cash. In the U.S., banks send checks back to the account holder after they are processed, so anytime you pay by check, you will get your "canceled check" back and it is your receipt. If you send cash in the mail, you probably won't get a receipt. Plus there is the possibility that your money will just disappear.

Page 87 D

1 They want to "pick up some chicks" – or at least Jay does. A nicer way to say the same thing is they want to meet some women.
2 No, not very. Jay doesn't take "no" for an answer, which in this case would be the only polite thing to do, and Meg says, "Get lost!" This is not at all polite.
3 He brings them two draft beers, which means

they are not bottled but from the tap.
4 She wants to "pick up" Mike and take him to her house. Mike doesn't want to go.
5 Because he hasn't met any women at this club – he says, "This joint's a real bummer." "Joint" is a slang word meaning "place." "A bummer" is something that makes you feel down or depressed.

Page 90

1 If you hate long tours, Mini Tours would be the best for you. Patriot II offers tours by boat. A Short Walk with History, the Streetcar Museum, the Top of the World and the Old Town Mall will all tell you something about the city's history. Tour Tapes would probably give you the most details about the city.
2 You can see old films at the Wheeler

Auditorium. If you are free at noon, you could go to the Center Forum. The Arena Players do theater, not opera.
3 The Planetarium is where you can learn more about the stars. If you enjoy night life, the Block is the place to go. The aquarium has lots of animals. The Museum of Art is for you, if you like art history.

Page 91 Activities

It's a breeze: It's very easy; *I'm into that:* I'm very interested in that; *I hear you:* I understand what you mean; *Got a light?:* Can you light my cigarette?; *That was a trip:* That was fun or surprising; *This joint's a real bummer:* This place is depressing; *Let's move on:* Let's leave and go somewhere else; *See you around:* Goodbye (I probably won't see you again); *Get lost!:* Go away! Leave me alone!

An *index* is a guide to the contents of a newspaper or book. (Indexes are at the back of a book or magazine, while the table of contents is at the front.) A *schedule* is a list of times when things are going to happen. A *commercial* is an advertisement on television or radio. An *intermission* is a break or pause in a performance. A *TV network* is a large company producing material for broadcasting by TV stations. A *TV station* is an establishment equipped for television transmission. A *hit* is a movie, book, song, play, etc., that is very popular and a success. A *bomb* is one that is not successful at all. A *guy* is a young man; a *chick* is a young woman. *Guy* is not negative or impolite usually, but *chick* is. *Draft* beer comes out of a tap; the other way to buy beer is in bottles, or *bottled*.

Test yourself

1 g; 2 a; 3 j; 4 f; 5 i; 6 h; 7 d; 8 e; 9 b; 10 c.

Using slang to talk about the opposite sex: 2, 3 and 8.

UNIT 10

Page 92 C

1 George Bates is.
2 He's leaving June 3rd and will be gone three and a half weeks.
3 You can stay with him for two or three days.
4 The best way to reach him is at work at the number (402) 894-2055.
5 Yes, it looks as if Kenneth Moore suggested you write to him. He is a mutual friend, that is, a friend of both yours and George's.

Page 93 D

1 Rose Alexis and Carl Matthews are the speakers.
2 They are in Minneapolis, Minnesota.
3 He's at a conference in the city.
4 Because Ron Apple in Tucson, Arizona, gave him their number and told him to call them.
5 They're going to have dinner together at the Alexis's house.
6 You could call or write a letter well in advance (at least two or three weeks ahead of time). You might ask if there's anything you should bring, such as blankets or a sleeping bag.

Page 93 F

1 No, she didn't.
2 They're going to a party.
3 She wants to see the old historic buildings and some old films.
4 She doesn't care for museums.
5 Joan offers to walk around the Old Town with her, to check the papers and get an International House film schedule for her and to help her do her laundry in her own machine.
6 No, Joan doesn't get Margo anything to drink. Margo gets it herself. Joan is not being impolite. In fact, she's being hospitable and showing Margo that she is a welcome guest and should make herself feel at home.

Page 94 B

1 San Francisco is the city she'll be visiting.
2 She'll fly on Pan American flight 612.
3 On Monday at 9:25 a.m.
4 Probably she's there on business for Robertson and Company. She's also hoping to see the San Francisco Bay area and see some art, so it's both business and pleasure.
5 She will be renting a car from National while she's in San Francisco. For the trip to Los Angeles she'll be taking a shuttle flight there and back.
6 At the Hyatt Regency Hotel in downtown San Francisco.
7 She's scheduled to be in meetings on Wednesday with the Japanese representatives, on Thursday with the presidential committee in Los Angeles, and on Friday there will be board meetings and concluding sessions in San Francisco.
8 On Thursday all morning.
9 She's particularly interested in art.
10 On Monday evening she is free; on Tuesday she wants to go to the ballet; on Wednesday she has no plans; on Thursday she has a choice of going to Chinatown or taking a boat to Alcatraz; on Friday she has planned to go to the theater to see the Berkeley Players at the University Theater in Berkeley; on Saturday her evening is still open.
11 Yes, it's probably being paid for by Robertson and Co, because it's a business trip.

Page 95 C

1 Tina will be going to art galleries the whole afternoon on Monday; she's planning to go to the Visual Arts Studio exhibit on Tuesday morning and to the modern art museum on Tuesday sometime after 2:00 p.m.; she's hoping to see the De Young Museum on Thursday between 2:00 and 4:30 p.m.
2 She should write in under Friday at 4:00 p.m. "golf with Larry."
3 Her heavy day and early night will probably be on Wednesday.
4 She will probably walk around town either on Monday or Tuesday. It sounds like she wants to be by herself, but she says it's because of her asthma, and presumably regular walking helps her to breathe better.

Page 96 B

1 Midway Motors is celebrating the opening of a new headquarters – probably a new complex of buildings and a new plant.
2 The event will begin at about 4:00 p.m. on Friday, October 10th.
3 It will be held at the new premises – north of Orlando, Florida, on Palma Road.
4 If it is not specifically mentioned on the invitation, it is assumed that you will wear coat and tie – or semiformal dress. Informal would be casual dress; formal would be tuxedo and evening gowns.
5 Yes, they ask you to tell them if you plan to come. "R.S.V.P." means please respond to this invitation by calling or writing to the secretary of the company.
6 Follow the map.

Page 97 D

1 Jean's party will be held outside.
2 It's a potluck dinner party. That means everyone brings something to eat.
3 No, she isn't. Americans often call each other by first names, even when they have just been introduced. If you aren't sure, you should listen to how other people address each other.
4 Yes, she does. She asks him if he's enjoying his visit to Memphis; she asks about his work and she asks where he's staying; she agrees with him about saving money on transportation; she offers him something to drink; she gives him her business card.
5 No, probably not. He says that he's afraid he'll have to take a rain check, which means that he'll gladly have something to drink another time or accept an invitation at a later date.
6 Yes, they'll probably meet again. When Alan says he'll be back in Memphis in 5 weeks' time, he suggests meeting with Lois then. Lois seems genuinely interested and shows it by giving Alan her card. Of course, it's possible that they are just being very friendly and that they won't follow up on it.

Test yourself

1 f; 2 j; 3 h; 4 b; 5 c; 6 g; 7 a; 8 d; 9 e; 10 i.
To make someone feel at home: 1, 3, 4, 5. To express that you don't want to do something: 6, 8.

Check yourself

Here are examples of things you could say in each of the nine situations:

2 At a restaurant: "Could we have the check, please, waiter?" or "We didn't order two Cokes, waiter. Could you please check our check again?"

3 At a hotel: "Hello! I'd like to check in, please."

4 At a bank: "I'd like to open a checking account, please." or "I have a check to cash."

5 At an airport: "I'd like to check in for my flight, please." or "Here is my luggage. Can I check it, please?"

6 At a gas station: "Could you check the oil, please?"

7 On a questionnaire: "Which box should I check?"

8 At a hotel: "I'd like to check out, please."

9 At a store, hotel, restaurant or bank: "Will you take a travelers check?" or "I'll sign my travelers check for you."

TAPESCRIPT

UNIT 1 ✈

Part 1 page 3   D. Listen and answer

You will hear a conversation at a Customs desk. Listen first and then answer the questions.

OFFICER: Okay, bags on the table, please. Your Customs form, please . . . uh-huh. How long you plannin' to stay in the country?
TOURIST: Four weeks.
OFFICER: Do you have anything to declare?
TOURIST: What?
OFFICER: Alcohol, cigarettes, . . .
TOURIST: No.
OFFICER: Any meat, fresh fruit, plants?
TOURIST: Uh, no.
OFFICER: Open your suitcase, please. Any gifts?
TOURIST: Excuse me?

OFFICER: Are you bringing any gifts into the country?
TOURIST: No, huh-uh.
OFFICER: Uh-huh. What's in the bottle?
TOURIST: Uh, hand lotion.
OFFICER: Okay, that'll be okay. Here's your form.
TOURIST: Uh, what should I do with it?
OFFICER: See that officer over there by the gate? He'll take it.
TOURIST: Thank you very much.

Part II page 5   C. Look and listen

You will hear three conversations at the airport. Looking at the map on page 4, figure out where the speakers are and where they have to go. Listen to the way people ask for and give directions.

1.
MAN: Excuse me! Could you tell me where the Eastern airlines counter is?
WOMAN: Sure. Just go up the escalator here on your left, and you'll see it next to the Continental counter when you get to the top.
MAN: Thanks a lot.
WOMAN: You're welcome.

2.
CLERK: Here's your ticket. Your flight's now boarding at Gate 62.
CUSTOMER: Excuse me?
CLERK: Gate 62.
CUSTOMER: Uh, where is Gate 62?
CLERK: Go down Concourse L, to your left there. You'll see it.

CUSTOMER: Down Concourse L? Thank you very much.
CLERK: You bet.

3.
FIRST MAN: Excuse me. Do you know where the baggage claim area is?
SECOND MAN: Yeah, it's downstairs. Take an elevator at the far end of the hall there, and it'll be right behind you when you get downstairs.
FIRST MAN: Okay, let's see . . . I take that elevator down there and turn around when I get to the first floor and I'll see it.
SECOND MAN: Right.
FIRST MAN: Great! Thanks.
SECOND MAN: Any time.

UNIT 2 ☎

Part 1 page 13   D. Listen and answer

You will hear three phone conversations. A man is trying to make a long distance call. He calls Directory Assistance first. Listen first and then answer the questions.

1.
OPERATOR: What city, please?
VICTOR: Chicago.
OPERATOR: Go ahead, please.
VICTOR: Yeah, do you have a number for a Henry Banks?
OPERATOR: There's an H. J. Banks on North Lincoln Park West and an H. S. on South Lasalle.
VICTOR: It's the one on Lincoln Park West.

OPERATOR: That number is 478-4620.
VICTOR: 478-4620. Thanks.

2.
OPERATOR: What number did you dial, please?
VICTOR: 478-4620.
OPERATOR: That number's been changed. The new number is 528-7825.
VICTOR: Okay, thanks.

3.

OPERATOR: Please deposit $3.00.

HENRY: Hello?

VICTOR: Hey, Henry! How are you doin'? This is Vic. I'm callin' from Baton Rouge.

HENRY: Vic! Far out! Great to hear from ya, man! What's up?

VICTOR: Well, I'm going to be in Chicago this weekend and I thought we could get together. Going to be there?

HENRY: Sure. Why don't ya give me a call when you get into town?

VICTOR: Will do. See ya Saturday!

HENRY: All right. Bye-bye!

Part II page 15   C. Look and listen

You will hear four conversations on the phone. Listen to the way people ask for information and take and leave messages. Listen to the conversations again and figure out who the speakers are, and whether or not they know each other.

1.

CALLER: Let's see. Information is 555-1212 . . .

OPERATOR: What city, please?

CALLER: I beg your pardon?

OPERATOR: What city, please?

CALLER: Yes, Miami, please. I want to know the weekend rate from Chicago.

OPERATOR: I'm sorry, but I don't have that information. You'll have to call the operator.

CALLER: Oh. How do I do that?

OPERATOR: Hang up and dial 0, ma'am.

CALLER: Dial 0 . . .

OPERATOR: Operator.

CALLER: Yes, I want to call Miami and I need to know how much it costs on Friday night.

OPERATOR: Did you check your directory, ma'am?

CALLER: Well, yes, but I couldn't find it.

OPERATOR: Hold on . . . It's 39 ¢ plus tax for the first minute and 27 ¢ plus tax for each additional minute till 11:00. After that it's 26 ¢ and 18 ¢.

CALLER: Thank you.

2.

TERRY: Ayers Travel. Terry speaking. May I help you?

SHERRY: Yes, I'd like to speak to Mr. Bixby, please.

TERRY: I'm sorry, but Mr. Bixby's tied up at the moment. He's on another line. Can I take a message, or would you like to hold for a moment?

SHERRY: Well, . . . I'm calling long distance from Dallas . . . Tell him Sherry Snyder, with a "y," of Standard Oil called, please, and I'll try to reach him again later on.

TERRY: Fine, Ms. Snyder, I'll do that.

SHERRY: Thank you. Goodbye.

3.

ANN: Hello?

WALLY: Hi! Is Tod there?

ANN: Tod? No, he isn't. Is this Wally?

WALLY: Yeah. I just wanted to know if he's still going to play tennis with me tomorrow.

ANN: Oh, hi, Wally. Yeah, as far as I know he is. Want him to call you back?

WALLY: Sure, thanks. Tell him I'll be home all evening.

ANN: Will do. Bye now.

WALLY: Bye.

4.

RECORDING: Hi. This is Jean Thompson's answering machine. I'm sorry I'm not in at the moment, but I'll get back to you if you just leave a message and a number at the sound of the tone. Thanks.

UNIT 3

Part 1 page 23   D. Listen and answer

You will hear a conversation that takes place at a car rental agency at the airport. Listen first and then answer the questions.

AGENT: Hi! May I help you?

FERRIS: Yes, I reserved a car and I'd like to pick it up. My name's Ferris, F-E-R-R-I-S.

AGENT: Okay . . . yes, here we are.

FERRIS: Uh, could you tell me again what kind of car I ordered? I'm afraid I forgot.

AGENT: Certainly . . . a Chevy Citation.

FERRIS: Oh, yes, now I remember. You know, I really don't need such a big car now, because I'll be traveling alone. Would there be a smaller one available, by any chance? It'd be nice to have one that gets better gas mileage.

AGENT: Well, I'm not sure, but I can check. How long will you be needing it?

FERRIS: Until Friday.

AGENT: All right . . . No, I'm sorry, but there's nothing available here at the airport. I'll check our downtown office, if you like.

FERRIS: Oh, no, that's all right then. If only I had reserved a Honda or something from the agent

in Europe, but I'll take the Citation.
AGENT: I'm sorry we can't help you further, but the Chevy gets good mileage. Could you just sign here, please? Will that be cash or charge?
FERRIS: Charge. Do you take Visa?
AGENT: That'll be fine. Sign here please.
FERRIS: Okay. Uh, where is the car rental area located?

AGENT: Okay, just take the pedestrian underpass down there on your right and take a left when you get to the other end. You should bring the car back to the same place on Friday, and just leave the keys in it.
FERRIS: Thank you very much.
AGENT: Have a nice trip!

Part II page 25   C. Look and listen

You will hear three conversations that take place at a car rental counter. Listen to the way people ask for information about their rental agreement. Looking at the form on page 24, find the information they're talking about and decide what the customer has to do.

1.
AGENT: Is that all then?
CUSTOMER: Uh, no – could you tell me what I should do if the car breaks down?
AGENT: Well, I'm sure you won't have any trouble, sir, but if something should happen, just call this number. They'll see that you get help.
CUSTOMER: Thanks very much.

2.
AGENT: Do you have a question?
CUSTOMER: Yes. I'm reading the agreement and I don't see . . . Could you show me where the part about insurance is?

AGENT: Of course – here, these boxes.
CUSTOMER: Oh, yes, thanks.

3.
AGENT: Is there anything else?
CUSTOMER: Yes, I'd like to know what to do in case of accident.
AGENT: Mmm-hmm. At the bottom of the form you'll see that you are expected to notify the police in the town where you are, and you have to fill out one of *our* forms, too. You'll find some in the car.
CUSTOMER: Thanks. I hope I don't need them!
AGENT: So do I!

UNIT 4

Part 1 page 33   D. Listen and answer

You will hear two conversations that take place on a city bus and in a taxi cab. Listen first and then answer the questions.

1.
RICHARD: Do you go to the University District?
DRIVER: Yup. Put your 55¢ in the fare box.
RICHARD: Oh . . . I've only got quarters. Can you change one for me?
DRIVER: Didn't you see the sign? Exact change only.
RICHARD: Oh . . . Uh, say, do you have change for a quarter?
MAN: I dunno. Let me check my pocket . . . Uh, yeah, here you go. Two dimes and a nickel.
RICHARD: Thanks!
MAN: Sure, any time.

2.
DRIVER: Did you call a cab?
LADY: Yes, I did.
DRIVER: Okay, where to, lady?
LADY: The Twilight Room?
DRIVER: Uh, is that the one in the Riverview Hotel?
LADY: No, it's at the corner of 5th and Market downtown.
DRIVER: Oh, sure, I know where that is. I'll have you there in no time.
LADY: Fine.

Part II page 35   C. Look and listen

You will hear two conversations at a bus depot. Listen to the way people offer to do something and the way other people turn them down.

1.
CUSTOMER: How much is a ticket to Reno, please?
CLERK: Forty-two fifty one-way, eighty bucks even round trip. You see, there's a savings if you get the round trip. You want it?
CUSTOMER: No thanks. Just one-way, please. I'll

be going on from there later.
CLERK: Oh, well, in that case you could get a ticket to wherever you're goin' after that, or you could get one of our thirty-day passes.
CUSTOMER: Thanks very much, but a one-way ticket to Reno is all I need today.

CLERK: Okay, it's up to you. A one-way to Reno, then.
CUSTOMER: Yes, thanks.

2.
CLERK: Here's your ticket, ma'am.
CUSTOMER: Thank you. Uh, can I check my suitcase?

CLERK: Sure can. Just carry it out to the bus and the driver'll take care of it for you.
CUSTOMER: All right.
MAN: Excuse me, I'll take it for you, if you like.
CUSTOMER: No, thank you, I'm fine. It's not very heavy.
MAN: If you say so.
CUSTOMER: Thanks anyway.

UNIT 5

Part 1 page 43   D. Listen and answer

You will hear two conversations. A man is calling to reserve a room in a motel. Listen first and then answer the questions.

1.
CLERK: Caravan Hotel, good evening.
JIM: Hi! I was wondering if you have a double room for tonight?
CLERK: Oh, I'm sorry. I'm afraid we have no vacancies at this time.
JIM: Okay, thanks anyway.
CLERK: You might try the Flamingo Motel. It's near the airport on Sandy Boulevard.
JIM: Okay, thanks.
CLERK: Any time.

2.
CLERK: Good evening, Flamingo Motel.
JIM: Yes, I wanted to know if you have a double room for tonight?
CLERK: Yes, we do.

JIM: Oh, good! Do you have one with a waterbed?
CLERK: Let me check . . . yes, we do, for $45 a night.
JIM: Yes, that'll be fine. Can you hold it for me? My name's Goldschmidt.
CLERK: Yes, I can hold it for you until 6:00 with no obligation on your part. Do you know how to get here?
JIM: Yes, I do, thanks. It should take us about twenty minutes, I think.
CLERK: Fine, Mr. Goldschmidt. We'll have the room for you.
JIM: Thank you. Bye.
CLERK: Goodbye.

Part II page 45   C. Look and listen

You will hear three conversations at the Red Lion Inn. Listen to the way people ask to have things done.

1.
CLERK: Ah, good morning, Mrs. Scott. What can I do for you?
WOMAN: Good morning. I've got a suit I'd like to have cleaned by tomorrow. Could you see to that?
CLERK: Yes, the hotel has a laundry and cleaning service. There's a laundry and cleaning slip in the room for you to fill out. Just leave the suit in your closet with the laundry slip where the maid can see it. Or you can give it to her if you see her. Your suit should be back to you in the morning.
WOMAN: Wonderful! Thank you.

2.
MARSHA: Come in!
MAID: Excuse me. Will you be leaving soon or can I do the room now?
MARSHA: Oh, yes, come right in . . . By the way, this blouse needs to be ironed. Could you see that it gets done?

MAID: Well, no, we don't have a pressing service here.
MARSHA: Oh, I see. Is there an iron I could use, then?
MAID: Yes, ma'am, there's one in a room down at the end of the hall. Just help yourself.
MARSHA: Okay, which way is it?
MAID: To the right and down past the elevators.
MARSHA: Thanks.

3.
CLERK: Yes, may I help you?
MAN: Yes, my name's Lund, room 1522. I'd like to have a meeting room scheduled for me this afternoon at 2:00. Can you take care of that?
CLERK: Yes, sir, I'm the one to see. How many people will there be?
MAN: Let's see . . . there'll be six of us.
CLERK: Okay, Mr. Lund, Room B, down the hall behind you, second room on the right.
MAN: Thank you.

UNIT 6

Part 1 page 53   D. Listen and answer

You will hear a conversation at a bank. Listen first and then answer the questions.

TELLER: Next, please . . . Hi, can I help you?

ROBERT: Yes, I hope so. I'd like to buy some travelers checks. Can I pay for them with a Eurocheque?

TELLER: A Eurocheque? I'm not sure . . . let me ask my supervisor . . . Yes, that'll be fine, as long as you have proper identification.

ROBERT: Of course. Here's my passport. I'd like to write two checks for fifty pounds each. All right?

TELLER: Fine. Just make them out to the First Community Bank of Colorado Springs. Now, travelers checks . . . what denomination would you like – fifty, twenty, or ten dollar checks?

ROBERT: Twenties will be fine. What's the service charge?

TELLER: It's two percent.

ROBERT: Okay.

TELLER: All right, here you are. Sign each check here on this line. I'll have your change in a minute.

ROBERT: Fine, thank you.

Part II page 55   C. Look and listen

You will hear three conversations in the telegraph office. Listen to the way people ask how long it will take to do things.

1.

AGENT: Next please. What can I do for you?

ARTHUR: Yes, I'd like to wire some money to my son in Albuquerque, but I don't have any cash with me. How do I go about it and what's the upper limit?

AGENT: Well, just take this money order form and fill it out. You got a credit card on you?

ARTHUR: Sure.

AGENT: Well, you can wire up to $1,000 with this form.

ARTHUR: Okay . . . uh, what do I put here where it says "ID. Question"?

AGENT: Just write in what you want your boy to answer before he's handed the money. Be sure to call him and give him the right answer!

ARTHUR: Okay. How long will it take for the money to get to Albuquerque?

AGENT: I s'pose it'll be there by this evening if we send it regular.

ARTHUR: Oh, that'll be fine.

2.

AGENT: Can I help you?

JOHN: My parents are wiring some money from Washington state. How long'll it take to get here?

AGENT: It should be here by tomorrow, but maybe not until the next day. It depends on how they send it.

JOHN: I see. I won't need it until this weekend, so I'll check back with you Friday.

AGENT: Fine.

3.

AGENT: Next please.

VALERIE: Hi. How long does it take a telegram to get to Fort Worth?

AGENT: Well, that depends on what kind it is. A regular telegram would be there by this afternoon, and a night letter by tomorrow.

VALERIE: This doesn't have to be there until tomorrow, so a night letter would be fine.

CLERK: All right.

UNIT 7

Part I page 63   D. Listen and answer

You will hear three conversations. In the first one, a man is calling a restaurant to reserve a table. The second and third ones take place at a restaurant. Listen first and then answer the questions.

1.

MAÎTRE D': Good evening, Le Cuisinier.

MR. NOVAK: Hello. I'd like to make a reservation for next Saturday night.

MAÎTRE D': All right. How many are there in your party, sir, and what time would you like to come?

MR. NOVAK: At 7:30, and there'll be four of us.

MAÎTRE D': Just a moment, please . . . I'm afraid I don't have anything for four at 7:30. Would 8:00 be all right?

MR. NOVAK: Yes, it would.

MAÎTRE D': Your name, please.

MR. NOVAK: Novak.

MAÎTRE D': All right, Mr. Novak, I've reserved a table for a party of four at 8:00 this coming Saturday.

MR. NOVAK: Thank you. Goodbye.

MAÎTRE D': Goodbye.

2.

WOMAN: Oh, it's lovely!

MAN: Mmm, it smells wonderful! Shall we find a table?

WOMAN: No, the sign says "Please wait to be seated," so someone'll come and show us to a table. Here she comes now.

HOSTESS: Good evening. Two?

MAN: We're expecting two more in a few minutes, so there'll be four of us.

HOSTESS: Then I'm afraid it'll be about ten minutes before I can seat you. Would you like to have a cocktail in our lounge while you're waiting?

WOMAN: Oh, yes, let's do that.

HOSTESS: I'll let you know when your table's ready.

3.

MARY: Excuse me, would you mind not smoking?

PAUL: Oh, I'm sorry, I didn't realize it was bothering you. I'll just finish this cigarette . . .

MARY: I'd appreciate it if you'd put it out now. I'm allergic to smoke.

PAUL: All right, all right, you win lady.

Part II page 65   C. Look and listen

You will hear three conversations in the restaurant. Listen to the way people ask the waiter about things on the menu.

1.

WAITER: Have you decided, sir?

CUSTOMER: Not quite. What's chicken teriyaki?

WAITER: It's white meat – boneless chicken breast – marinated in a brown sauce that's a little bit sweet, and char-broiled for just a few minutes so it's still juicy. It's really very good.

CUSTOMER: It sounds good, all right. I'll take your word for it and try some.

WAITER: All right, one chicken teriyaki.

2.

WAITER: May I take your order?

CUSTOMER: I think so . . . What are the stuffed mushrooms like?

WAITER: They're mushrooms filled with bread

and cheese mixed with herbs and spices, and then baked. They're served warm. Would you like to try some?

CUSTOMER: No, thank you. I'll just have the sirloin, medium-rare, please.

3.

WAITER: Are you ready for dessert?

CUSTOMER: Yes, I believe so. What's your cheesecake like?

WAITER: It's a very rich and creamy cheesecake, and comes with whipped cream on top. Can I bring you a piece?

CUSTOMER: Oh, yes, that sounds delicious.

UNIT 8

Part I page 73   D. Listen and answer

You will hear three conversations. In the first one, a woman is sick in bed at home. The second and third take place at the doctor's office. Listen first and then answer the questions.

1.

LAURA: Boy, do I feel awful. I've been sneezing all day, and I think I even have a fever.

VERN: Sounds like you're getting a cold, honey. Did you take some vitamin C?

LAURA: Yeah, I did. I *hate* colds! I hate having to carry Kleenex around, and have to worry about bacteria, and I don't like taking those cold tablets like Dristan or Contac.

VERN: Have you taken your temperature?

LAURA: Not yet, but I guess I should. Where's the thermometer? . . . Well, it's almost 101. I guess I have to face the facts.

VERN: Yeah, you should just stay in bed. Maybe we can keep it from getting worse if you're really coming down with something. I'll make you something hot to drink – you know you should have plenty of fluids. And I'll call your boss and say that you can't make it to the office in the morning.

LAURA: Thank you, dear.

2.

DOCTOR: Have a seat right here and open your mouth wide, please. Yes, your throat looks pretty sore. Have you taken anything for it?

KEITH: Yes, some aspirin yesterday. It didn't help much.

DOCTOR: Mmm-hmm. Have you had a cold or the flu lately?

KEITH: No, I haven't.

DOCTOR: There's a bad virus going around and that's probably what it is. But I'm going to take a throat culture so we'll know for sure. But it'll be a couple of days until we get the lab report back. Are you allergic to any medication?

KEITH: Not that I know of.

DOCTOR: Okay, just sit tight. I'll be back in a minute.

3.

NURSE: Can I help you?

ROGER: Yeah, I have hay fever and I left my medicine back home in Phoenix. I was wondering if the doctor could give me a prescription for some?

NURSE: Not without examining you first. You might want to come back later or make an appointment. No? Well, you'll just have to wait

till he has time to see you.

ROGER: How long'll that be?

NURSE: There are several people with appointments before you, so I guess it'll be at least an hour before it's your turn.

ROGER: Okay, I'll wait.

NURSE: Well, just take a seat in the waiting room, then.

Part II page 75   C. Look and listen

You will hear three phone conversations with people who are not feeling well. Listen to the way they ask and tell about health problems.

1.

BOB: Hello?

ANDY: Hi! This is Andy. How are you doing?

BOB: Not so good. I've got the flu.

ANDY: Oh, I'm sorry to hear that. What kind of flu is it?

BOB: Stomach flu. You know, terribly upset stomach, nausea, vomiting – yesterday I couldn't even keep warm water down.

ANDY: That sounds awful. Is there anything I can do?

BOB: No, I don't think so. Peg's taking care of me. I just have to wait until it's over.

ANDY: Well, I hope it doesn't take long. Let me know if I can help.

BOB: Okay, I will. See you.

2.

DORIS: Hello?

CAL: Doris? This is Cal Farley from the office. I heard you were ill.

DORIS: That's right. It was appendicitis. I had some very sharp stomach pains a few days ago, so they put me in the hospital for observation for a day. Then they decided to operate.

CAL: I'm sorry it was so serious. How are you feeling now?

DORIS: Pretty good, considering. I'll probably be back at work next week.

CAL: Well, I'm glad to hear that. Let us know if there's anything we can do.

DORIS: Thank you, I'll do that.

3.

FRANK: Hello?

ELLEN: Hi! This is Ellen. I heard you'd been in an accident, so I thought I'd call and see how you're doing.

FRANK: I'm not feelin' too hot. I got a broken ankle, two broken ribs. I'm stiff and sore and bruised all over, and my head still aches like hell. Aside from that I'm doin' real well! Just been lyin' around in bed all day feelin' sorry for myself. The doc says I might as well forget about the World Cup next weekend.

ELLEN: Well, at least you still got your sense of humor!

FRANK: That's about all I got.

ELLEN: You want me to come over?

FRANK: Sure. I need some cheering up.

ELLEN: Okay, I'll be over this afternoon.

UNIT 9

Part I page 83   D. Listen and answer

You will hear a conversation that takes place in a married couple's home. The woman's parents are visiting. Listen first and then answer the questions.

GREG: Gee, it's nice to have you here in Manhattan!

MR. & MRS. WEBSTER: It's nice to be here!

GREG: What would you like to do this weekend?

MRS. WEBSTER: Oh, I don't know. It'd be nice to see a play or maybe a musical.

MONA: *If* we can get tickets.

GREG: That may be a problem, all right. Well, let's check the paper and see what there is . . . let's see, movies are on page 19, section 2, of the *Times*. Can you check that out, honey?

MONA: Sure.

GREG: Here's the theater section of the *Voice* . . . oh, there's a performance of *Rigoletto*

tomorrow night, and they apparently still have tickets.

MR. WEBSTER: Going to the opera is a little too fancy for me.

MONA: Oh, Dad, you don't have to dress up anymore. You can wear just about anything you want to these days.

MRS. WEBSTER: I'd rather see a musical, I think.

MONA: Well, the movie *Annie*'s playing not far from here.

MRS. WEBSTER: Mmm, that sounds good. I've never seen it.

MR. WEBSTER: But we should see something on stage while we're here in the city.

GREG: Well, I'll just call some box offices downtown and see what the ticket situation is.

MR. WEBSTER: Sure, that's a good idea. And while you're doing that, I think I'll check the TV schedule.

Part II page 85   C. Look and listen

You will hear three conversations. One of them takes place at the home of a friend, one at a hotel, and the third at a box office. Listen to the way people ask about what there is to do – especially about concerts.

1.

BRIAN: Richard?

RICHARD: Yes?

BRIAN: I think I'd like to hear some good classical music while I'm here, something by a large orchestra. As a musician, what would you suggest?

RICHARD: Well, there's always the Philharmonic. They perform regularly. And the Masterwork Chorus and Orchestra is featuring Handel's *Messiah* this week and next, I think. I can recommend that.

BRIAN: That sounds good, thanks. I guess I'll call and see about tickets.

RICHARD: Here's the paper. You can probably find their number under Concerts in the second section. It'd be a good idea to check with them right away, because they could be sold out already for this weekend.

2.

MAN: Excuse me.

HOTEL CLERK: Yes?

MAN: I wanted to see a rock concert while I'm in New York, but I don't know which groups are playing. Do you have any information, and could you recommend something?

HOTEL CLERK: Sure. The Police are supposed to be here at the end of the month, but I think I heard they're sold out. Then there's Rockpile and Moon Martin, and Boz Scaggs, who gives a great performance, and Dire Straits . . .

MAN: Did you say Dire Straits?

HOTEL CLERK: That's right.

MAN: Thank *you*! Where can I get tickets? I've always wanted to see them in concert!

3.

WOMAN: Hello.

BOX OFFICE CLERK: Yes, dear?

WOMAN: I'd like two tickets to Keith Jarrett for tomorrow night.

BOX OFFICE CLERK: What price would you like, dear?

WOMAN: Well, I don't know . . . I've never been here before, and I'd like good seats. What do you think would be best?

BOX OFFICE CLERK: There're some very good fourteen-dollar seats left, in the tenth row. The eleven-dollar ones are sold out, and the cheap ones are pretty good seats, of course – there's not a bad seat in the house – but they're not as good as the more expensive ones.

WOMAN: Well, okay, I'll take two fourteen-dollar tickets.

BOX OFFICE CLERK: You won't be sorry, dear.

WOMAN: Thank you, I'm sure I won't.

UNIT 10

Part I page 93   D. Listen and answer

You will hear a phone conversation. A man is calling a couple he doesn't know. Listen first and then answer the questions.

ROSE: Hello?

CARL: Hello, is this Rose Alexis?

ROSE: Yes.

CARL: You don't know me, but this is Carl Matthews. Ron Apple out in Tucson gave me your number and suggested I give you a call.

ROSE: Oh, that's nice. So you're a friend of Ron's? How is he anyway?

CARL: Oh, he's doing very well. Their new baby boy's a real tiger, and Ron's being promoted again. Lucy's planning to go back to work soon, and she's looking forward to that.

ROSE: Well, that's good to hear. Carl, what are you doing in Minneapolis?

CARL: I'm attending a conference at the Hilton until Thursday.

ROSE: Will you have any time at all to get together?

CARL: Well, tonight there's a banquet I have to go to. But tomorrow and Thursday evening I'm free.

ROSE: Good, why don't you come for dinner tomorrow? Do you have a car?

CARL: No, I'm afraid I don't.

ROSE: Well, I'll ask Bill to pick you up after work – say, at six? Then he can avoid the rush hour.

CARL: Sounds absolutely great! My room's 483, Carl Matthews. He can call me from the lobby and I'll come down.

ROSE: Fine. I'm looking forward to it!

CARL: Me, too. Until tomorrow, then.

ROSE: Bye.

Part II page 95   C. Look and listen

You will hear four conversations. Listen to the way people agree to suggestions – sometimes definitely and sometimes tentatively – and the way they sometimes try to get out of things politely. Look at the appointment calendar on page 94, so that you can see what days and times the speakers are talking about and where Tina will probably be at those times.

1.
JOHN: What are your plans while you're here?
TINA: I'll be spending most of my free time in the art museums.
JOHN: Well, the basketball championship's going to be on TV, you know. You don't want to miss that. It starts at seven tomorrow night.
TINA: I think I'm going to be busy, but I'll sure try to make it in time.
JOHN: Good, I really hope you can.

2.
LARRY: How much free time will you have between your business meetings?
TINA: Not much.
LARRY: Oh, that's too bad. I was hoping you'd have time for a game of golf.
TINA: I'd like that. Let's see . . . how about 4:00 on Friday? That's the last day of conferences. Is there a bus to the golf course?
LARRY: Friday's fine with me. I'm afraid the bus doesn't go out there, though. In fact, bus service is pretty poor in general in this town. It'd be better if I picked you up at your hotel. I can stop by on the way.
TINA: Fine.

3.
ROD: Hey look! The Cops are playing at the Downtowner tomorrow night. You doing anything? Want to go?
TINA: What kind of music do they play?
ROD: Rock 'n roll, honey, and lately they've been getting into hard rock. You got to hear them!
TINA: I'd love to, but don't think I can. After all the stuff they have on the agenda for me tomorrow, I'll probably just want to come home and take it easy. I'll see if I can get out of any of it, but don't count on me.
ROD: Okay. Just let me know in time.

4.
SAM: Want to drive around town and check out the main strip?
TINA: I'd really rather just walk around and take in some of it at my own pace. You know, the cafés, the crowds and all that. And with my asthma I need to get plenty of fresh air and exercise every day.
SAM: Okay, it's *your* vacation.

Weight

1 ounce (oz.)	=	28.35 g.
1 pound (lb.)	=	16 oz. or .45 kg.
2.2 pounds (lb.)	=	1 kg. (divide by 2 for kilos)
1 ton (t.)	=	2,000 lb. or 907.18 kg.

Liquid

1 tablespoon (T.)	=	3 teaspoons (tsp.)
½ fluid ounce (fl. oz.)	=	1 T.
1 cup (c.)	=	8 fl. oz. or .24 l.
1 pint (p.)	=	2 c. or .47 l.
1 quart (qt.)	=	2 p. or .95 l.
1 gallon (gal.)	=	4 q. or 3.79 l. (multiply by 4 for liters)
1.25 gallons U.S.	=	1 imperial gal. (British)

Length, Distance and Land Measure

1 inch (in. or ")	=	2.54 cm.
1 foot (ft. or ')	=	12 in. or .3 m.
1 yard (yd.)	=	3 ft. or .9 m.
1 mile (mi.)	=	5,280 ft. or 1.6 km.
1 acre	=	.4 hectares (ha.)

Temperature

	Fahrenheit (F)	Celsius (C)
freezing point	32°	0°
room temperature	61° – 71°	16° – 21°
body temperature	98.6°	37°
boiling point	212°	100°

$C° = (F° - 32) \times .55$

Several more short forms and abbreviations used in the U.S.A.

@	at the cost of (each)		M.D.	Doctor of Medicine
a.m.	before noon		memo	memorandum
apt.	apartment		mfg.	manufacturing
ASAP	as soon as possible		mgr.	manager
att.; attn.	attention		Mr.	Mister
bldg.	building		Mrs.	married woman (pronounced "misses")
co.	company			
c/o	care of, at the address of		Ms.	married or unmarried woman (pronounced "mizz")
CPA	Certified Public Accountant			
¢	cent		no.	number
dept., dpt.	department		Ph.D.	Doctor of Philosophy
̎	ditto, more of the same (used to refer to the item above it on a list)		pkg.	package
			p.m.	after noon
			PO	Post Office
Dr.	doctor		pres.	president
ea.	each		rec'd.; recd.	received
encl.; enc.	enclosed		rpm	revolutions per minute
govt.	government		temp.	temperature
GP	General Practitioner (doctor)		U.; Univ.	university
hr.	hour, hours		VIP	very important person
i.e.	that is		vol.	volume
inc.	incorporated		vs.	versus
I.O.U.	"I owe you" (some money)		w; w/	with
IQ	intelligence quotient		w/o	without
IRS	Internal Revenue Service		XL	extra large